**BOA**
EDITIONS LTD

# Little Mr. Prose Poem

## The Selected Poems of Russell Edson

T0005963

# Little Mr. Prose Poem

## The Selected Poems of Russell Edson

EDITED BY CRAIG MORGAN TEICHER

FOREWORD BY CHARLES SIMIC

AMERICAN POETS CONTINUUM SERIES, NO.196

BOA Editions, Ltd. ◊ Rochester, NY ◊ 2022

◊

Copyright © 2022 by The Estate of Russell Edson
Foreword copyright © 2022 by Charles Simic
Afterword copyright © 2022 by Craig Morgan Teicher

All rights reserved
Manufactured in the United States of America

First Edition
22 23 24 25 7 6 5 4 3 2 1

For information about permission to reuse any material from this book, please contact The Permissions Company at www.permissionscompany.com or e-mail permdude@gmail.com.

Publications by BOA Editions, Ltd.—a not-for-profit corporation under section 501 (c) (3) of the United States Internal Revenue Code—are made possible with funds from a variety of sources, including public funds from the Literature Program of the National Endowment for the Arts; the New York State Council on the Arts, a state agency; and the County of Monroe, NY. Private funding sources include the Max and Marian Farash Charitable Foundation; the Mary S. Mulligan Charitable Trust; the Rochester Area Community Foundation; the Ames-Amzalak Memorial Trust in memory of Henry Ames, Semon Amzalak, and Dan Amzalak; the LGBT Fund of Greater Rochester; and contributions from many individuals nationwide. See Colophon on page 176 for special individual acknowledgments.

Cover Design: Sandy Knight
Cover Art: "Structure" by Russell Edson
Interior Design and Composition: Michelle Dashevsky
BOA Logo: Mirko

BOA Editions books are available electronically through BookShare, an online distributor offering Large-Print, Braille, Multimedia Audio Book, and Dyslexic formats, as well as through e-readers that feature text to speech capabilities.

Cataloging-in-Publication Data is available from the Library of Congress

BOA Editions, Ltd.
250 North Goodman Street, Suite 306
Rochester, NY 14607
www.boaeditions.org
*A. Poulin, Jr., Founder (1938–1996)*

# CONTENTS

from *The Childhood of an Equestrian* (1973)

from *The Clam Theater* (1973)

from *The Intuitive Journey* (1976)

from *The Reason Why the Closet Man Is Never Sad* (1977)

from *The Wounded Breakfast* (1985)

from *See Jack* (2009)

◊

# FOREWORD

Prose poetry has been around since mid-nineteenth century and still no one has succeeded to this day to explain convincingly what it is. The usual definition states that it is poetry written in prose and leaves it at that. For most lovers of poetry, saying something like that is not just absurd, but a blasphemy against everything they call poetry. Free verse, of course, still has its detractors, but not many of them would go so far and insist that absence of rhyme and traditional prosody in Walt Whitman make the hundreds of poems he wrote over his lifetime prose and not poetry.

Anyone who was fortunate to hear Edson read his poems is not likely to have forgotten the experience. He made his audiences roar with laughter or sit astonished at what they were hearing. His heroes are dunderheads who resemble those we encounter in comic strips and silent film comedies with their dramatically simplified narratives which he learned from his father, Gus Edson, the famous cartoonist who created the character Art Gump.

Russell Edson was born in Stamford, Connecticut and lived there all his life, leaving home only to attend the Arts Students League in New York in his youth and in later years to give poetry readings in colleges and universities. He wrote his poems late at night in the attic of the home he shared with his wife Frances, while she slept in their bedroom below armed with a long pole which she used to knock on the ceiling whenever her husband's laughter got too loud and kept her awake.

Edson said that he wanted to write without debt or obligation to any literary form or idea. What made him fond of prose poetry, he claimed, is its awkwardness and its seeming lack of ambition. The monster children of two incompatible strategies, the lyric and the narrative, they are playful and irreverent. Not only did these "poems" not sound like anything one had ever read, but what went on in them was downright peculiar. "Let us consider the farmer who makes his straw hat his sweetheart," one of them begins. In another poem one reads about the rich hiring an orchestra and having the musicians climb into trees and sit on their branches to play happy birthday to their purebred dogs; there's also the one about a girl who teaches herself to play piano by taking it for a walk into the woods, and the one about a man who falls in love with himself and is unable to think of anything else but himself, being hugely flattered that no one else had ever shown him that much interest.

"A cast-iron airplane that can actually fly, mainly because its pilot doesn't seem to care if it does or not" is how Edson defined the prose poem. The real surprise comes when we realize that despite all the joking we are reading or listening to, these are not the scribblings of a village idiot, but of a comic genius and a serious thinker, as in this lovely little poem:

### Antimatter

On the other side of a mirror there's an inverse world, where the insane go sane; where bones climb out of the earth and recede to the first slime of love.

And in the evening the sun is just rising.

Lovers cry because they are a day younger, and soon childhood robs them of their pleasure.

In such a world there is much sadness which, of course, is joy…

— **Charles Simic, 2022**

from
## *The Very Thing That Happens (1964)*
◊

# Clouds

A husband and wife climbed to the roof of their house, and each at the extremes of the ridge stood facing the other the while that the clouds took to form and reform.

The husband said, shall we do backward dives, and into windows floating come kissing in a central room?

I am standing on the bottom of an overturned boat, said the wife.

The husband said, shall I somersault along the ridge of the roof and up your legs and through your dress out of the neck of your dress to kiss you?

I am a roof statue on a temple in an archaeologist's dream, said the wife.

The husband said, let us go down now and do what it is to make another come into the world.

Look, said the wife, the eternal clouds.

## When the Ceiling Cries

A mother tosses her infant so that it hits the ceiling.

Father says, why are you doing that to the ceiling?

Do you want my baby to fly away to heaven? The ceiling is there so that the baby will come back to me, says mother.

Father says, you are hurting the ceiling, can't you hear it crying?

So mother and father climb a ladder and kiss the ceiling.

## The Cruel Rabbit

A cruel rabbit quit its nest and came into the house of the old woman who takes medicine for dinner.

Her husband said, the cruel one is here.

The cruel one came in and bit the old woman. The old woman hit the cruel one with a fly-swatter until the cruel one was quite dead.

About this time another cruel rabbit was quitting its nest for the house of the old woman who takes medicine for breakfast.

# The Wheel

A mother awoke her son and said, go down and hurt your father.

Can't I do it tomorrow? I was just having a dream in which I was revenging myself against you, he said.

You can dream tomorrow, the mother said.

So the son went down and tied a wagon wheel to his father's neck.

I am not a vehicle, get this dirty thing off of me, said the father, for as you see I am writing a history of your mother.

The son yawned and went upstairs again.

He heard his father below: Get this wheel away from me quickly, as his father crawled with the wheel dragging from his neck. He heard his father scream: I do not want to write the history of the Wheel... Get this wheel away from me or I shall not be responsible for its safety.

Help help help, I cannot get away from a wheel. A wheel drives me crazy. A wheel has spokes which ray out of the hub to the rim.

Help, I am beginning to fall in love with a wheel—I court a wheel because a wheel is to be courted—I marry a wheel—We live happily ever after.

Help, help, I cannot get away from a wheel.

The son heard his father sighing: I am set out with a wheel. I go down the road with a wheel. I do not ride a wheel, I drag it because it will not stand up, as it is enraptured with me as my wife is not; that it clings to my neck as I crawl through the dust of the road.

## The Very Thing That Happens

Father comes riding into the kitchen on an imaginary white horse. Mother mother, look at my heroic head work, screams father as he beats his head with a horse whip.

You are doing something, she says.

Yes yes, mother, and that is how it is done; my head's a horse, and I have invented a new head which is head number two; where my intrinsic head, which is left head number one, resides.

I don't like it one bit, roared mother.

But you see, but you see, my intrinsic head lives in my left buttock as head number two. Oh, it is great fun, mother, it is great fun, screamed father.

Yes yes, turning around I see you—Looking around a doorway I see you, roared mother.

Yes, see me, see me, screams father.

Why is what is what? yells mother.

It is like my head thinks of a horse and becomes a horse, screams father, because how else does it happen when a head becomes a horse?

But why why why is it happening? cries mother.

Because of all things that might have happened this is the very thing that happens.

## Dialogue for Father and Son

A father and son live in a wood and have animal heads. The father's head is a bird's head and the son's head is a dog's head.

 We are two persons aren't we, father? said the son.

 There are two persons where we happen to be, said the father.

 I have a head like a dog because I am not a dog; is that how it is, father? said the son.

 In the same way, said the father, that a dog has a head like a dog because he is not a man.

 And so of birds as regards your head? asked the son.

 So of birds, as they are not my sons though they think I am their father, said the father.

 Then it is as though two persons were in a wood? said the son.

 Yes, it is likely that two persons are in a wood, said the father.

 And that of the two persons there is one with a bird's head and the other with a dog's head? said the son.

 Yes, but the birds are not my sons though they take me for their father; my son has a dog's head, said the father.

## Going Upstairs

How a man can go upstairs. He will put a ladder against a wall; but the ceiling is in the way, and he bumps his head because he goes up headfirst. Like the time when he was born, he had preferred to put one toe out first, but he went headfirst.

His father sitting below the ladder said, why are you doing this terrible thing?

Because I'm going to the second story because I know the first by heart.

So he is bumping his head, and he is trying again; and each time he bumps his head. And his father is saying, I don't like your head, and that ladder turns my stomach.

The ceiling has a way of always being in the way.

Will you please, said his father, take the stairway.

Where father, where, into the woods by the lake?

No no, walk up the stairs.

Ah ha, and you promise the ceiling hasn't overgrown the stairwell; and I won't have to bump my head all day to attract your attention?

If my attention is attracted I promise to look out of the window.

## Waiting for the Signal Man

A woman said to her mother, where is my daughter?

Her mother said, up to you and through me and out of grandmother; coming all the way down through all women like a railway train, trailing her brunette hair, which streams back grey into white; waiting for the signal man to raise his light so she can come through.

What is she waiting for? said the woman.

For the signal man to raise his light, so she can come through.

# The Fetcher of Wood

An old man got into a soup pot and shook a wooden spoon at the sky.

When he had finished he went upstairs to his room and died.

When his wife came home she said, stop being dead, there is no reason for it.

He got out of bed. So you're dead, what of it? she said. I have no patience with you today—Go fetch wood for the stove.

He collapsed onto the floor. Oh, go along with you, you can at least fetch some wood. She kicked the corpse to the stairs and over the edge, and it fell to the first floor. Now, fetch wood, she screamed.

The corpse dragged itself out of the door. Spiteful old man, she said to herself, died just to get out of fetching wood.

The old man's cadaver was trying to chop wood. The ax kept slipping out of its hands. The cadaver had cut off one of its legs below the knee.

Now the cadaver came hopping on one leg into the kitchen, carrying its leg. Oh, you've cut my old man's leg off, she screamed. And she was so angry that she fetched the ax and began to chop up the corpse—Chop your leg off to get out of work, will you?—Die when I need you to bring the wood in, will you? ...

The old man, leaning over a cloud, watched the old woman chopping up his corpse—Give it hell, baby, give it one for me...

When the old woman had finished, she gathered up the pieces and put them into a soup pot—Now die to your heart's content—And tell me you can't fetch wood...

## A Condition

A man has put his bedroom in order; he has swept and made his bed. Now he sits by the window waiting for it to be night. But it is still early morning and his father wants him to leave home. So that a man finds nothing else to do except to remake his bed and re-sweep his bedroom; and then to sit by the window and wait for the night.

But still his father wants him to leave home.

So that a man feels if he parts his hair down the middle of his head and slicks his hair flat against his head the sunlight might reflect from it into his father's eyes.

But his father still wants him out of the house.

This is a condition that lasts for thirty or so more years.

# For a Time

A man decided not to stand up anymore, and so he crawled on his hands and knees. He did not have the bad feeling any more.

He would crawl around the house on his hands and knees from room to room. Or sometimes just stand on his hands and knees in the middle of a room looking at a wall; or tilt his head and look at another wall. And then slowly crawl to another room...

One time he put his hands on a windowsill and looked out of a window; and then he dropped his hands back to the floor and looked into the wall below the window for a time.

Anytime he felt tears on his cheeks he would stand still for a time.

He would crawl to the empty fireplace and look into it. And sometimes he would crawl to a chair and put his head under it for a while.

But if he felt any wet on his cheek he would be still for a time.

And sometimes he would shut his eyes and crawl backward until his feet touched a wall; and there he would remain until such time as he crawled forward again.

## A Stone is Nobody's

A man ambushed a stone. Caught it. Made it a prisoner. Put it in a dark room and stood guard over it for the rest of his life.

His mother asked why.

He said, because it's held captive, because it is the captured.

Look, the stone is asleep, she said, it does not know whether it's in a garden or not. Eternity and the stone are mother and daughter; it is you who are getting old. The stone is only sleeping.

But I caught it, mother, it is mine by conquest, he said.

A stone is nobody's, not even its own. It is you who are conquered; you are minding the prisoner, which is yourself, because you are afraid to go out, she said.

Yes yes, I am afraid, because you have never loved me, he said.

Which is true, because you have always been to me as the stone is to you, she said.

## When Something is Broken

When something is broken, you cannot fix it. You have taken a hammer to it, but you cannot fix it. You have banged and banged, and still it is not fixed. You have tried to mend it with your tears, but they are not thick enough. You have tried again with the hammer, and broken it only further.

Was it then that the authority removed you from your difficulty and broke you in the house of understanding?

It is from the window, there with your back to the room, looking out that you know that tears cannot mend; no matter how intent or tender, tears are not enough...

from
*What A Man Can See (1969)*
◊

## Dream Man

Dream man said he will do dreams. He has a box and a clock. He has a clock to wind when it is Wednesday.

An apple is very cherry bigger, it is very something the same.

And dream man said he will do dreams, He will do boxes—Now can you hide there, yes you can. And the clock which can go tick.

If somebody who loves you does not love you and there is very nothing to do like you will wind on Wednesday or apple as a cherry is as is an apple as a cherry.

Can you hide, I think so. Can you think so, I think so. In a box to hide. Can you do a box like you can a dream if somebody who loves you does not love you.

You can do a dream like she loves you.

Dream man will dream he is not dreaming and dream himself awake and wind his clock which makes it Wednesday and he has a box.

## What a Man Can See

There was a tower where a man said I can live. After grief it can happen that he comes. Then he saw summer its field and its tree. He heard the wind and he saw a cloud.

# A Man Had a House

A man had a house here he did not live but watched it as he loved it its walls and that we might have come together there, and loved it for it was sheltering with wall paper and the household stuffs.

He lived in grass because it is well to cleave the sight on blades and to watch as windows brood or smear with moon.

And he wondered who lived in that house. It was a cup he knew lived in that house with a chair.

And he wondered who lived in that house and so lived he in grass wondering. And wondered who he was and he is grass attendant in decor to the house.

But was this enough. Should not one go out for sports like a war between the south and north poles which is like to compress the earth like a head with both head and chin hair, oh anything to do.

A man has a house which is to have. And when lights go on yellow oblongs at night if not moon smear or star streak.

The man eats grass because he has a friend who is a cow, in his head.

But his friend is turning into a man and he into a cow.

And he is a cow with a man in her head and doesn't know why she thinks of a man and so forgets.

Then he wakes up again eating grass which he does not like without vinegar and oil/but he is a cow and loves to eat grass.

But then he wakes up again and runs as he sees his house has gone away to live in a neighborhood that he has never heard of, and has allowed a cow to come into its bedroom and be comfortable, and to sit at a window to look out.

And for the cow therefore to wonder if it will rain.

# Father and Son Traveling

A man had a sack which he kept father in. As he stood in the doorway of mother's house in silhouette with the sack over his shoulder, mother said, I see you are humpbacked, which is well, like the mother is the son, a flattery which is also echoed in our chin hairs, in our similar balding.

No, no, mother, my humped back is father...

Yes, your father was a humpback with chin hair, bald because he is of the family, flattering me by every loss and gain of his aging body; when his hair went so went mine, it was a morning not quite like this night, yet not quite dissimilar to be that different; but to go on, we had been sleeping, yes, and weeping, as was our way, also reaping, as was our way, the harvest that the dream is yielding; but when the morning came we found all our lovely hair on the pillow. It is my hair, said your father, as he gathered it up and spilled it on his head. And then the door opened and the wind came in and gathered it like a tumble weed and took it away. We stood at the door and watched the lovely silver stuff go down the road.

But I have father here in this sack, we have been traveling.

How nice for father and son to find the earth round or flat, or how you say, humpback, growing your chin hair, no matter where, it keeps coming out like your whole head was full of it.

Father wishes to blow you a kiss through the sack.

Wait son, I shall have to put some underwear over my face to keep discretion and modesty, while well admitting it is most flattering to have a person with chin hair demonstrate his affection... I think it better though if he did nothing, rather thought of my nude body discreetly inside his head.

He is now thinking of your nakedness, mother, which is a fine picture for the father to take on the road as he travels with the son. Goodbye, mother.

Yes, yes, goodbye, hello...

## The Road

There was a road that leads him to go find a certain time where he sits.

Smokes quietly in the evening by the four legged table wagging its (well why not) tail, friendly chap.

Hears footsteps, looks to find his own feet gone.

The road absorbs everything with rumors of sleep.

And then he looked for himself and even he was gone.

—Looked for the road and even that...

# The Fall

There was a man who found two leaves and came indoors holding them out saying to his parents that he was a tree.

To which they said then go into the yard and do not grow in the livingroom as your roots may ruin the carpet.

He said I was fooling I am not a tree and he dropped his leaves.

But his parents said look it is fall.

# The Singing Daughter

Does the daughter sing, said mother Moo.

The daughter did a song all about how the sun gets on things, like a roof and a side wall and into a window and on a man who cried: The sun is kneeling through a window on my forehead —Stop kneeling your golden knee through my window…

Daughter, I do not like that tune which have a melody I do not understand, as it makes my eyes hurt, and they are doing a bleeding all over my cheeks. (A man by a window should draw the shades)…So why does a daughter sing…

Because, said daughter, the earth was once silent until it became noised by persons.

And those poets did not do nothing to keep it quiet so you could get some sleep, neither—Which is they did not let nothing alone. But they repeated until you got very nervous and had to ask what the trouble was. Which is everything's got trouble —And why they don't stop making more I cannot understand, said mother Moo.

The daughter did another song: There was a tree that sucked back its twigs into branches, and its branches into boughs, and them into its trunk, and also its roots into its trunk. And its trunk shrunk into nothing. And there was no more tree. And it never was anyway.

Why wasn't it, asked mother Moo.

Because nothing is if it isn't until it is— Which is another song: There was once a house which had a door between the livingroom and the kitchen, which was an interior door which somebody wonders about, having only been in the kitchen…

That is a sad song, said mother Moo, that is the saddest song of all…

Here is a father-song for dad: There was once a man who looked into the corner of a room, and he saw the corner of a room, screamed daughter.

That is the prettiest of the songs, said mother Moo.

Here is a mother-song: There was a woman wearing an apron. She sat down on a chair and put the apron over her head. And so there was a woman with an apron over her head, screamed the daughter.

Let me kiss your foot-port for that delicate outburst of loveliness, roared mother Moo.

Another son, dear mother: There was a ball that had green on it, that was all alone in a big dark night, screamed the daughter.

O that is a lovely sonnet, roared mother Moo.

It is not a sonnet...

It is so...

It is not...

It is too, you dirty bitch, roared mother Moo.

## Something to Tell People

An old woman who loved to have something to tell people wondered what she could tell someone. She gave a loud scream to make sure her equipment was working.

And now she would test her mental thing, where the thinking is done. She hit her head with the heel of her hand trying to knock something loose.

She screamed again to make sure her noise maker was still working.

But she couldn't make a thought.

Shall she just scream in somebody's face and flail her arms about? Perhaps they'll think she's trying to say something. It's better to be thought of as trying to say something rather than just standing there mute.

She screamed again.

All she could think of was, a rat stole my foot and put it on and took a long walk. But the foot hurt the rat because the old lady's foot has a bunion.

No no, a rat stole the hair off my head for its nest. But father rat said, no no, take that away before I sneeze.

Or a rat kissed the heel of her foot and she had a blister there.

No no, she has rat whiskers growing out of her upper lip.

She screamed again.

from
*The Childhood of an Equestrian (1973)*
◊

# Antimatter

On the other side of a mirror there's an inverse world, where the insane go sane; where bones climb out of the earth and recede to the first slime of love.

And in the evening the sun is just rising.

Lovers cry because they are a day younger, and soon childhood robs them of their pleasure.

In such a world there is much sadness which, of course, is joy...

# Ape

You haven't finished your ape, said mother to father, who had monkey hair and blood on his whiskers.

I've had enough monkey, cried father.

You didn't eat the hands, and I went to all the trouble to make onion rings for its fingers, said mother.

I'll just nibble on its forehead, and then I've had enough, said father.

I stuffed its nose with garlic, just like you like it, said mother.

Why don't you have the butcher cut these apes up? You lay the whole thing on the table every night; the same fractured skull, the same singed fur; like someone who died horribly. These aren't dinners, these are post-mortem dissections.

Try a piece of its gum, I've stuffed its mouth with bread, said mother.

Ugh, it looks like a mouth of vomit. How can I bite into its cheek with bread spilling out of its mouth? cried father.

Break one of the ears off, they're so crispy, said mother.

I wish to hell you'd put underpants on these apes; even a jockstrap, screamed father.

Father, how dare you insinuate that I see the ape as anything more than simple meat, screamed mother.

Well, what's with this ribbon tied in a bow on its privates? screamed father.

Are you saying I am in love with this vicious creature? That I would submit my female opening to this brute? That after we had love on the kitchen floor I would put him in the oven, after breaking his head with a frying pan; and then serve him to my husband, that my husband might eat the evidence of my infidelity...?

I'm just saying that I'm damn sick of ape every night, cried father.

# The Complaint

When my big girl, Lucy Ann John, whom I had raised from a mere pup, fell out of the window, I at once rushed to my doctor book seeking an antidote.

The prophylactic is a parachute, or large springs tied about the body, mattresses placed below, or a net held by firemen.

But, no no, I want a cure!

It says in the doctor book: If the fall is very deep nothing is to be done for the first infection; however, the secondary infection, grief, is cured by leaping after the beloved.

## Composing a Love Song

We are having trouble controlling an umbrella, which has come to life.

We turn to ourselves, looking out of mirrors, for answers. But our images only repeat our questions.

Should the umbrella be destroyed? We have no way of telling what sort of food it will require. We cannot tell where its mouth will appear. Why does it not attack?

We think it must be a flying creature, and must fly when its hunger has gathered its full emptiness.

We are rather sure the hook of its handle will lift and carry things away.

Perhaps it dives with its sharp point foremost, stabbing its pleasure.

We discover that the umbrella is actually an ancient creature, known as the Umbra reptilis, and is descended from the great family of flying snakes. The root forgotten as man tamed these snakes into harmless sun shades and rain shelters. In the Dictionary of Familiar Spirits it is also noted that the favorite food of the Umbra reptilis is the rain-drenched Homo sapiens.

This strikes us as being rather odd... And we begin to understand why umbrellas, paradoxically, are used to shield men from the rain; for in the very use of the animal one is freed from its attack...

Now that we know that we are safe, there is no harm in using our energies to compose love songs to the umbrella.

There is no reason not to love.

# The Dainty One

I had remained in bed longer than it usually takes one's fatigue to drain off.

Very often there is a song one must sing the whole night through; it repeats, and there is no stopping it. One beats it out with one's canine teeth, or one's toes. It is a musical tic.

I have heard it said that it is a message that one dares not hear. In the dark the unconscious is a dangerous thing. I prefer "Melancholy Baby" to what else I might hear. And so I listen all night to "Melancholy Baby," gnashing each syllable with my teeth.

One feels that things are about to change. I have felt this all my life. It is a readiness that robs every act of meaning, making every situation obsolete, putting the present into the past.

A man is a series of objects placed in a box, the sound of a train, the sounds of his own liquids trickling through the intimate brooks of his body, a certain number of bones, tree shadows that fall through the flesh as nerve patterns, or blood vessels; pourings, exchanges, disconnections…

Improvisation mounted in a piece of meat, lying abed in the night. "Melancholy Baby" over and over. Slowed. Out of time… each syllable again and again…

## Dismissed Without a Kiss

A tired cow went into her barn and took off her milk bag and horns, and put them on a shelf.

She kicked off her hooves and detached her tail, and dropped her ribs and back legs to the floor.

She took her head off —Ah, that feels good! she sighed.

When the farmer came to tuck his cow in for the night he cried, my God, what has happened to my cow?

Oh goodnight! said the cow's milk bag.

What do you mean goodnight—Are you dismissing me without a kiss? cried the farmer.

## The Distressed Moth

A moth had gorged itself on mother's hair one night. Mother awoke to the sound of belching. Mother looked at the moth and said, why are you belching?

The moth belched at her.

Stop belching, said mother.

Father said, why is the house full of belches?

A moth is belching, said mother.

Why is a moth belching in someone's bedroom? cried father.

It has distress, said mother.

And why is there no hair on your head? said father.

Because the moth ate one of my spit curls, and then said, oh I will have just one more; and then still another, and even another, until the moth is really quite distressed.

I see, said father, but it's very poor taste to belch; and I regard it as proof of very poor breeding, which now takes vent; and having cast this first veil off must move towards even greater immodesties.

The moth belched again.

Mother, I won't be able to sleep if the moth continues to belch, cried father.

There there, said mother, I've heard you belch too.

Oh fine, that's a nice thing to bring up at a time like this, cried father.

But didn't you belch last Tuesday? said mother.

Here I'm trying to instruct the moth, and you undermine my authority by pointing up my digestive difficulties, cried father.

But you also farted, said mother.

Oh that was just a little aside which I thought you hadn't heard, sighed father.

The moth farted.

Now see what you've done! screamed father.

## An Extrapolation

I dressed the cow in my wife's wedding gown, simply that the cow, in spite of previous commitment to milk pail or butcher's block, might seem the lonely bride who, but for her genetic inheritance, was soon joined by the groom.

Yes, I extrapolate love's first night on a bed of hay. Yet my poor cow dressed in my wife's wedding gown thinks hay is food, and stands there munching her wedding veil mixed with hay, genetically imprisoned from the symbol of her gown.

Suddenly a chicken flew at the cow. The cow began to low with fear.
No no, bad chicken, I cried.

I was forced to dress the chicken in Uncle Henry's smoking jacket.
Soon the ducks and chickens were dressed in all the clothes of my relatives.
When I ran out of clothes I was forced to kill.
When I ran out of those who were to be killed I started on the others.

My wife asked me what I was doing in the barn, and I didn't know.

# A Letter from an Insomniac

Dear Mr. Furniture-Maker,

The bed you have made for me is a very difficult one. When I pull on its reins it rears up protesting the road.

And it seems to fear heights, for when I ask it each night to jump from the window, it hesitates.

It is impossible to sleep in a bed that is afraid of heights... I dream so often of the mountains.

I believe this bed is a valley creature.

## Piano Lessons

There was once a girl who was learning to play piano by taking it for walks in a wood.

She would guide it with an elephant goad.

Mother would say, oh do be careful, it's such a costly piece of furniture.

The piano farted.

Father said, take that horrible old man out of here or I shall really have to remember who I am, for I shall be shouting in such a manner as to be quite unlike myself.

But in time the piano became the greatest girl-player in all the world.

Father said, how odd.

Mother said, oh my.

The piano used an elephant goad in quite such a manner as to bring the girl to song.

It is quite lovely, said father.

It is not unlovely, said mother.

Very soon the house was filled with little pianos.

Father said, well, I hardly expected this.

And mother said, well, this was really not quite expected, but past the initial shock one learns to expect what has already happened.

## The Retirement of the Elephant

An elephant of long service to a circus retired to a small cottage on a quiet street, to spend its remaining days in the study of life after death.

It had looked forward to these quiet years, when the mind would be readied for the coming collapse of the biology.

But the elephant found that it was too big to fit through the front door. The elephant pushed through anyway, smashing the front of the cottage. As it started upstairs to the bathroom it fell into the cellar.

The elephant climbed out and went to the back of the cottage and broke in again, pushing down the remaining walls.

Now the elephant realizes that its only course is to run amuck—Yes, just to run amuck!

Goddamn everything!

## The Toy-Maker

A toy-maker made a toy wife and a toy child. He made a toy house and some toy years.

He made a getting-old toy, and he made a dying toy.

The toy-maker made a toy heaven and a toy god.

But, best of all, he liked making toy shit.

from
*The Clam Theater* (1973)

◊

# The Agent

... Assigned to you when your flesh was separating from your mother's, this shadow, who seeing the opportunity at hand, joined your presence, in such a way as some say the soul is given.

You have always caricatured me in my travels. I have seen you on mountains, and in dim cafes. I have seen you hold your head, your elbows on your knees; and while I was sad you were serene!

I seek a mastery over fate, of which you are, in objective witness, the agent of... I run away one night as you sleep, the trusting wife, whose borders have opened in the universal dark.

She feels in the morning among the sheets for the easy habit of her husband's shape—Now arc the earth, sweet dark, the law of umbra give you panic to search me out with your cunning speed of light!

# The Ancestral Mousetrap

We are left a mousetrap, baited with cheese. We must not jar it, or our ancestor's gesture and pressure are lost, as the trap springs shut.

He has relinquished his hands to what the earth makes of flesh. Still, here in this mousetrap is caught the thumb print of his pressure.

A mouse would steal this with its death, this still unspent jewel of intent.

In a jewel box it is kept, to keep it from the robber-mouse; even as memory in the skull was kept, to keep it from the robber-worm, who even now is climbing a thief in the window of his eye.

## The Avalanche

A weeping woman heard a slight roar.

Her tears had loosened the flesh of her cheeks and caused a small avalanche.

My goodness, she said as her left nostril fell out of her head.

But this only caused her to weep beyond even the first cause of her weeping.

My goodness, she said, now that I have something to really weep about it's ruining my face, and the more it ruins my face the more I have something to weep about.

My goodness, I must stop this weeping, even my lachrymal glands have fallen.

Soon her whole face fell. The plop of it startled her.

My goodness, she said.

# The Case

Your case...?

Mine, which is the only excuse I give for opening it.

You are opening it.

Yes, it is opened by me, which is the only excuse I give for opening it.

And it has things inside of it....

Yes, things are inside because I have put them there, each in its own recess.

Instruments?

Yes, an old shoe which people will say is simply an old shoe. It is in my case to associate its presence with this gingerbread man.... Then too, this rock, which is also to be noticed....And this toy sailboat....

These are things in your case.

These are things in my case. When I close my case they are still there. When I open my case I can see that. Because they are there they have probably been there all the time the case was closed.... I guess at this. I am confident that I shall not reverse my opinion. I am very well satisfied that what I have believed is so. I have made no contingency plans.

Then you are sure?

I am filled with confidence. I am closing my case because I have finished having it open. I am relatching its latch because I have concluded its excuse for being open by closing it.

Then it's closed...?

Yes, because I have done that to it.

# The Clam Theater

They had started a hat factory... Basically in a dream... Entirely so when you think that the very foundation begins somewhere in the brain, when the brain is unlaced like a shoe, and like a shoe free of the conscious foot with its corns and calls.

An old brick factory full of men mad for making hats rises in the head like Atlantis once more above the waters.... It is remarkable how like a foot the head really is; I mean the toes, perhaps ornaments of hair; the hollow of the arch must certainly find its mouth, the heel is already a jaw....

This is my theater. I sit in my head asleep. Theater in a clam....

Amidst the wet flesh of the head madmen build hats; perhaps to lay cover over the broken mind; or to say the head is gone, and all it is is hat.... Only hats hung on the hooks of our necks....

# Colic

The baby does not keep its brain; we keep finding it on the floor by its crib.

Grandmother is asked if a jackknife might be drawn through her hair; for it is known that the aged carry luck in the ancient silver of their curls.

Grandmother says, yes, but take care, for not only is luck stored there, but also the ornament that vanity celebrates.

Yes yes, Grandma, we would only burnish the instrument, to whet its appetite for luck, while vanity sleeps in the dreams of praises passed.

And so the instrument is readied in Grandma's luck, losing her only a few of the silver curls; gladly given, so we hope, to cure the baby's colic.

We pry open one of the fontanels with the father's jackknife, pressing the baby's brain into its head, hoping that it takes root, or however else it secures itself under the bone; and, perhaps in that solitary confinement, that darkness, find those few attitudes properly appraising this world.

But even so, the baby throws up its brain again. And we conclude old hair carries no special luck, only the flowers of a vanity, worked slowly over the years into ornaments of silver.

Father says, let us pray.

# The Cradle

*for Jonathan*

Because it made my grandmother seem older I was not allowed to become any older myself; and spent my life in a large cradle, big enough for a man, shaking my rattle and teething ring for grandma's smile.

One day after practicing for years I said, please let me grow up, grandma dearest.
Do you want to kill me, wretch, with your self-indulgence?
And so I waved my teething ring at her, and she smiled.

Sadly enough this did not save her life.
I have remained in this large cradle, big enough for a man, waiting for grandma to smile at me again.
I shake my rattle at night, it sounds like the fire of distant stars.

## Elephants

A herd of elephants stands in the yard, old pieces of tusk lying in the grass at their feet.

They endure through winter and summer, slowly evolving their monumentality.

It is said that the eye of a fly can actually see the hour hand moving.

The body collects itself gradually from carrots and chops; works late into the night, translating these things into fingernails and pubic hair.

The night is falling, and nature sucks its teeth at my window. I pretend to be living my own life.

## The Family Monkey

We bought an electric monkey, experimenting rather recklessly with funds carefully gathered since grandfather's time for the purchase of a steam monkey.

We had either, by this time, the choice of an electric or gas monkey.

The steam monkey is no longer being made, said the monkey merchant.

But the family planned on a steam monkey.

Well, said the monkey merchant, just as the wind-up monkey gave way to the steam monkey, the steam monkey has given way to the gas and electric monkeys.

Is that like the grandfather clock being replaced by the grandchild clock?

Sort of, said the monkey merchant.

So we bought the electric monkey, and plugged its umbilical cord into the wall.

The smoke coming out of its fur told us something was wrong.

We had electrocuted the family monkey.

# The Floor

*for Charles Simic*

The floor is something we must fight against. Whilst seemingly mere platform for the human stance, it is that place that men fall to.

I am not dizzy. I stand as a tower, a lighthouse; the pale ray of my sentiency flowing from my face.

But should I go dizzy I crash down into the floor; my face into the floor, my attention bleeding into the cracks of the floor.

Dear horizontal place, I do not wish to be a rug. Do not pull at the difficult head, this teetering bulb of dread and dream....

# The Mental Desert

The mind is mostly desert. The moon is lovely there, and almost turns the sands to water, save for one's natural logic.

At the paper-doll factory we are issued scissors, and warned not to monkey with our wrists.

I am an extremely serious person, needing no lectures on the care and maintenance of my tools.

I let the wrist business go unchallenged. Why should I invite discourse about monkeys with inferiors who, though in executive station, are nevertheless inferiors in the art of the scissors.

One's work involves the folding of paper, snipping here and there, and finally unfolding a self-portrait of insomniacs in a line of beds, each a night, arranged end to end.

Another ingenious design is a traffic of cars joined bumper to bumper, and so on, depending on how many folds one has made.

One dependable old woman with a rather unlovely stare creates a masturbator pattern: a chain of lonely men holding their penises, ingeniously attached penis by penis; one long spit through all their groins.

There is the morning-bus motif, the public-toilet motif, any number of old favorites.... Yet, I thought to give the factory a motif closer to the popular taste; and by this means prove myself worthy of executive station. I created a suicide motif: a chain of paper-doll factory workers attached elbow to elbow, cutting their wrists.

An inferior foreman merely said, you are well on your way to the misuse of your tools, which may well involve your monkey.

... My monkey? I screamed.

... Of course the mind is a desert; one grows used to the simplicity of thirst.

## My Uncle in the Distance

My uncle had a mustache made of spinach. It was green and full of sand. It was lovely in the distance when one had lost sight of it among the leaves of trees.

But at close range, particularly at the dinner table, it seemed something caught on his upper lip, which he should have had the decency to lick off.

But my uncle doesn't like spinach, especially when it's so full of sand.

Poor uncle, finally in complement to his mustache, slowly gave up his animality. Soon it was no longer uncle, but a hodgepodge of squashes and root plants, leafy and fungal portions, waddling about the house.

Until father cried, my God, cut him up for supper!

After that the difficulty seemed to disappear into the distance of the years... lovelier and more distant each of the years that are the distance they create.

## The Nostril Affair

His left nostril was visiting in his right nostril. And he was feverishly swatting flies hoping that one of the flies was not a fly but the dark of his missing nostril.

At last despairing he drew a dark spot on the left wing of his nose with a pencil.

Suddenly his left nostril crawled out of his right nostril, and he saw that he had three nostrils.

He erased the extra one.

He heard a scream.

My God, my God, I've killed a nostril.

The dead nostril fell to the floor.

His other nostril crawled up into his nose. Even the pencil mark edged out onto his cheek pretending to be a beauty spot.

He called to the nostril hiding in his nose, oh please come out, it was all an accident.

He even called to the pencil mark, please do not be afraid, I will buy you an ice-cream cone....

# Oh My God, I'll Never Get Home

A piece of a man had broken off in a road. He picked it up and put it in his pocket.

As he stooped to pick up another piece he came apart at the waist.

His bottom half was still standing. He walked over on his elbows and grabbed the seat of his pants and said, legs go home.

But as they were going along his head fell off. His head yelled, legs stop.

And then one of his knees came apart. But meanwhile his heart had dropped out of his trunk.

As his head screamed, legs turn around, his tongue fell out.

Oh my God, he thought, I'll never get home.

# The Pleasure of Old Age

When you get old you come apart. Your elbows become frayed, and bones begin to show. Your knee caps are as bare of flesh (too much love), as your head, of hair (too much thought).

And as you are dressing one day one of the nipples comes off your chest, and drops to the floor like a shirt button. The old woman sews it back, remarking how like paper is the skin of your chest; she is sure the stitching will tear out.

You save your toes in a bottle, they are always breaking off in your shoes; they look like teeth.

One morning as you sit for your daily stool you are not surprised to see that you have delivered your purple liver into the toilet; and a broken tube from your lower bowel hangs from your anus.

When you get old your dry and cracked ribs stick out of your chest. You break them off like kindling.

The old woman is constantly coming to sew your lip or ear back on. She complains your skin just won't hold the thread.

She sews your penis and scrotum on, but the thread breaks through the flesh. It just won't come right, she says.

Still, you enjoy her fussing with your penis.

from
## *The Intuitive Journey (1976)*
◊

# How Things are Turning Out

*for Michael Cuddihy*

A man registers some pigeons at a hotel. They fly up to their rooms. He's not sure that his mind doesn't fly with them...

He asks the desk clerk if everything seems all right. He would like to know if the smoke coming out of his cigarette is real, or something the management has had painted on the wall?

The desk clerk has turned his back and is sorting the mail.

Sir..., says the man.

But the desk clerk continues to arrange the mail.

Sir, would you look this way for a moment?

I can hear you, I'm just sorting the mail.

I wanted you to notice the smoke of my cigarette... Since the pigeons flew up to their rooms... You never know about the future, I mean how things will finally turn out... Please, could you check my smoke...?

When the desk clerk turns his face is covered with hair, like the back of his head; and the front of his body is like the back of his body.

Where is your front?

My twin brother has the fronts; I was born with two backs... I always got the spankings... But why regret the past?

That's good philosophy...

My best subject.

... Tell me, is everything turning out all right?

So far so good...

# Counting Sheep

A scientist has a test tube full of sheep. He wonders if he should try to shrink a pasture for them.

They are like grains of rice.

He wonders if it is possible to shrink something out of existence.

He wonders if the sheep are aware of their tininess, if they have any sense of scale. Perhaps they just think the test tube is a glass barn...

He wonders what he should do with them; they certainly have less meat and wool than ordinary sheep. Has he reduced their commercial value?

He wonders if they could be used as a substitute for rice, a sort of woolly rice...

He wonders if he just shouldn't rub them into a red paste between his fingers.

He wonders if they're breeding, or if any of them have died.

He puts them under a microscope and falls asleep counting them...

# The Abyss

A dining room floats out into space…

On earth a cook with a large ham turns back. She calls across the abyss to the living room where people are waiting for dinner, sirs and ladies, I can't get the ham into the dining room…

Has the Cook suddenly developed a sense of humor?!
… I don't think's she's so funny.

Sirs and ladies, I can't get the ham into the dining room… Shall I try the split soup? Maybe I could get some bread in…? I'll try…

Just get the food on the table, and stop trying to be funny!
… I don't think she's so funny.
No no, I didn't mean she was successful, I meant she was trying to be funny.
Well, that's something, lots of cooks won't even try…

Sirs and ladies, I can't even get the bread into the dining room. Perhaps I could slip a few olives in…? I'll try…

What in hell is she trying to pull?!—Olives?!—She'll try to slip a few olives in?! You'd better just cut the excuses, and get the dinner on the table!

Sirs and ladies, I can't find the dining room; I don't think it's in the house.

… Not in the house?! Have you ever heard of anything so silly?

She's certainly not clever, but she is trying, you've got to give her that.
But she wasn't hired to entertain us.
… Do you really think she is entertaining?
No no, I didn't mean she was entertaining, but for some odd reason she's trying to be. Perhaps she wants a raise…?
Well, at least that's more than most cooks'll do, they all want raises; but

how many of them really try to be entertaining?

Sirs and ladies, what shall I do…?

Try singing; so far your performance is not very good!
… Can she sing?
Who knows? She's tried everything else, we might as well hear her sing…

## The Feet of the Fat Man

The fat man is asked why he's so fat.

He claims to be only as fat as he needs to be; he doesn't think he's overdoing it…

How does one measure? Just being fat seems too much. On the other hand, accepting that there are fat people, how can one tell when a fat man is too fat?

Yet, this man is so fat that his head suddenly slips down into his neck. His face looks up out of his neck. He says, what do you think, do you think I'm overdoing it?

Now his shoulders and chest are slipping down into his stomach and hips—oh my God, he's beginning to fold down like porridge into his thighs!

He's definitely too fat, his bones won't support it.

God, he's going into his calves! His ankles are beginning to bulge.

When he finishes he's only a couple of feet all swollen out of shape.

In one of the feet where the ankle should start is his face. He says, what do you think, do you think I'm overdoing it?

We look into the other foot just to make sure he doesn't have another face; and we are pleasantly surprised to see hair, the foot is full of hair; which we take to be the other half of his head, the back half…

# Time of the King

There was a king who didn't like to wait very much. When a pleasant date was approaching he would simply do away with the days or weeks that stood between.

ALL CITIZENS ARE ASKED TO X ALL THE DAYS ON THEIR CALENDARS BETWEEN NOW AND THE KING'S PLEASURE.

At other times the king might insist on re-playing a particular date representing some high satisfaction: IT WILL BE MAY 13, 1974 FOR TWO WEEKS, OR UNTIL FURTHER NOTICE.

Sometimes the king, in moods of having nothing to look forward to, would reverse the calendar to dates of former pleasures. Sometimes he would remain in the past for years.

One day he settled into childhood, just on the edge of puberty, just when he was discovering the joys of masturbation.

No no, that looks bad, said one of his high advisors.

What's so bad about a kid having a little fun? Freud says it's normal, said the distracted king.

After a year of masturbating the king became very depressed and decided he didn't want to live anymore.

The king consulted insurance company actuarials, had medical advice as to his general health, checked the longevity of his ancestors, and put all this through a computer, arriving at a date when he might reasonably expect to die of *natural* causes; had new calendars printed describing a year many years away; and specifying a month and day in that future year, went to bed and died.

# A Roof with Some Clouds Behind It

A man is climbing what he thinks is the ladder of success.

He's got the idea, says father.

Yes, he seems to know the direction, says mother.

But you do realize that some men have gone quite the other way and brought up gold? says father.

Then you think he would do better in the earth? says mother.

I have a terrible feeling that he's on the wrong ladder, says father.

But he's still in the right direction, isn't he? says mother.

Yes, but, you see, there seems to be only a roof with some clouds behind it at the top of the ladder, says father.

Hmmm, I never noticed that before, how strange. I wonder if that roof and those clouds realize that they're in the wrong place? says mother.

I don't think they're doing it on purpose, do you? says father.

No, probably just a thoughtless mistake, says mother.

Then their son reaches the top of the ladder and is shouting down to his parents, mommy, daddy, success!

Do you think we should tell him? says mother.

No, let him enjoy it while he can, says father.

Then mother shouts up to her son, enjoy it while you can, honey.

While I can? he shouts down.

While you still don't notice that it's only a roof with some clouds behind it, she shouts.

Okay, he shouts down, while I still don't notice that it's only a roof with some clouds behind it I'll enjoy it while I can.

And remember, son, you can always go into the earth! screams his father.

# Mr. & Mrs. Duck Dinner

An old woman with a duck under her arm is let into a house and asked, whom shall I say is calling?

Mr. and Mrs. Duck Dinner.

If you don't mind my asking, which is which?

Pointing to the duck the old woman says, this here's my husband.

A little time passes and the butler reappears, yes, come right in, you're expected, the kitchen's just this way.

In the kitchen there's a huge stove. The butler says, I'm sorry, we don't have a pot big enough for you, so we're using an old cast-iron bathtub. I hope you don't mind? We have a regular duck pot for your husband.

No no, this is fine. I'll make pretend I'm having a bath.—Oh, by the way, do you have enough duck sauce? says the old woman.

Yes, plenty, and the cook's made up a nice stuffing, too.

My husband'll need plucking; I can undress myself, says the old woman.

Fine, that'll be a great help; we'll have the kitchen girl defeather your husband.—By the way, what would you suggest with duck? asks the butler.

Wild rice, but not too wild, we wouldn't want any trouble in the dining room; and perhaps asparagus spears… But make sure they're not too sharp, they can be quite dangerous, best to dull them on a grinding wheel before serving…

Very good, Madam.—By the way, do you think that having the kitchen girl defeather your husband might be a little awkward, if you know what I mean? She is rather pretty, wouldn't want to start any difficulties between you and your husband, says the butler.

No worry, says the old woman, we're professional duck dinners; if we start fooling around with the kitchen help we'd soon be out of business.—If you don't mind I'd like to get into the oven as soon as possible. I'm not as young as I used to be, not that I'm that old, but it does take me a little longer these days…

# The Hemorrhoid Epidemic

They kill the man's monkey because they think it has infected the neighborhood with hemorrhoids.

The man thinks the monkey too good to waste, even if there is only enough monkey to make one boot.

And so he has one boot made, and calls this his monkey-boot.

The boot reminds him of his monkey; the fur on it is exactly like the fur on his monkey.

But, why not, he thinks, is it not made from the same monkey whose fur is like the fur on his boot?

But since there is only one boot he decides he'll either have to have one of his legs amputated or have the boot made into a hat.

He decides to have the boot made into a hat because he has only one head and will not have to have one of his heads amputated.

But when the boot has been made into a hat he doesn't know whether to call it his boot-hat or his monkey-hat.

The hat reminds him of a boot he once had.

But why shouldn't it, he thinks, was it not once a boot?

But that boot reminds him of a monkey he once had.

Yet, why should it not, he thinks, was it not made from the same monkey that it reminds him of?

He is puzzled.

Meanwhile, the hemorrhoid epidemic continues to spread…

# The Marionettes of Distant Masters

A pianist dreams that he's hired by a wrecking company to ruin a piano with his fingers...

On the day of the piano wrecking concert, as he's dressing, he notices a butterfly annoying a flower in his window box. He wonders if the police should be called. Then he thinks maybe the butterfly is just a marionette being manipulated by its master from the window above.

Suddenly, everything is beautiful. He begins to cry.

Then another butterfly begins to annoy the first butterfly. He again wonders if he shouldn't call the police.

But, perhaps they are marionette-butterflies? He thinks they are, belonging to rival masters seeing whose butterfly can annoy the other's the most.

And this is happening in his window box. The Cosmic Plan: Distant Masters manipulating minor Masters who, in turn, are manipulating tiny Butterfly-Masters who, in turn, are manipulating him... A universe webbed with strings!

Suddenly it is all so beautiful; the light is strange... Something about the light! He begins to cry...

## Grass

The living room is overgrown with grass. It has come up around the furniture. It stretches through the dining room, past the swinging door into the kitchen. It extends for miles and miles into the walls...

There's treasure in grass, things dropped or put there; a stick of rust that was once a penknife, a grave marker... All hidden in the grass at the scalp of the meadow...

In a cellar under the grass an old man sits in a rocking chair, rocking to and fro. In his arms he holds an infant, the infant body of himself. And he rocks to and fro under the grass in the dark...

# The Captain's Surprise

*A Film Script*

The ship is ready. I step aboard. *(Keep the camera on me.)*

The Captain, a poor actor, is applauding a sea gull for the remarkable feat of flying over his ship. Did you see that? he cries. Nature has finally invented a creature that can fly!

I have myself seen the gulls fly many times; and I wonder at the legitimacy of the Captain's surprise. *(I hope you have the right lens, this is a close-up.)*

I wonder if the Captain has the proper license for surprise? And even if he has, whether it's up to date and properly stamped by the Commissioner of Surprises?

Perhaps the Captain merely tries to draw the camera away from me?

Even so, one must wonder how he handles the great iceberg that looms in front of our ship one night.

Does he hold his cocktail in front of his drunken eyes and see only another piece of ice floating in his glass?

Something is happening below deck. *(Have the camera pan down into the galley to pick up the cook having intercourse with a large pile of fresh dough.)*

*(In closing, pull the camera up into the clouds. Show the whole ship. To give the picture a sense of motion make sure the wake is full of white foam; if necessary, this can be painted in later.)*

from
*The Reason Why the Closet Man Is Never Sad* (1977)
◊

# The Adventures of a Turtle

The turtle carries his house on his back. He is both the house and the person of that house.

But actually, under the shell is a little room where the true turtle, wearing long underwear, sits at a little table. At one end of the room a series of levers sticks out of slots in the floor, like the controls of a steam shovel. It is with these that the turtle controls the legs of his house.

Most of the time the turtle sits under the sloping ceiling of his turtle room reading catalogues at the little table where a candle burns. He leans on one elbow, and then the other. He crosses one leg, and then the other. Finally he yawns and buries his head in his arms and sleeps.

If he feels a child picking up his house he quickly douses the candle and runs to the control levers and activates the legs of his house and tries to escape.

If he cannot escape he retracts the legs and withdraws the so-called head and waits. He knows that children are careless, and that there will come a time when he will be free to move his house to some secluded place, where he will relight his candle, take out his catalogues and read until at last he yawns. Then he'll bury his head in his arms and sleep… That is, until another child picks up his house…

## The Cliff

... Standing on a cliff overlooking the sea, sea gulls like scraps of paper blowing over the rocks below. A steady north-east wind, at first refreshing, the chilling; storm coming...

An old fisherman wearing rubber boots makes his way along the cliff. He is carrying something on his back; it is supported by a line over this shoulder which he clutches in his hands. It seems to be a large fish.

On closer inspection it turns out to be an old woman, the line coming out of her open mouth. I imagine a fishhook stuck in her throat.

The old fisherman stops and lets the old woman slide off his back to the ground. Storm coming, he says. He nods in the direction of the old woman on the ground, my wife.

Is she dead? I say, trying to sound concerned.

Oh no, just resting; we always take our walk along the cliffs.

He puts his fingers in her mouth and removes the hook from her throat. There ya be, he sighs.

His wife sits up and yawns; she says, looks like a storm coming.

The old fisherman puts the hook in his mouth and swallows it. And now the old woman picks up the line and begins dragging the old man away. His eyes are shut.

I see the old woman struggling with the line over her shoulder, dragging what seems to be a large fish, as she makes her way through a fine rain just beginning to fall.

# The Coincidental Association

Dr. Glowingly turned to Dr. Glisteningly and said, why are you copying everything I do?

But why are you copying everything I do? replied Dr. Glisteningly.

We can't both be copying, cried Dr. Glowingly.

But I deny it! screamed Dr. Glisteningly.

One of us is copying the other, said Dr. Glowingly.

Admittedly, conceded Dr. Glisteningly, the piling up of coincidence is far too great; either we are both being controlled by a third party, which I rather disbelieve, or one of us is being cued by the other.

I believe you are unconsciously imitating me—no more of it! Dr. Glisteningly; I will not have my spontaneity blurred by your constant echo, said Dr. Glowingly.

Why, look at you, wearing the same deerstalker cap as I wear, the same gray spats, cried Dr. Glisteningly.

Well, it's no secret that I admire your taste—why shouldn't I, isn't it in direct imitation of mine? said Dr. Glowingly.

Perhaps we will not prove who is the copycat, but I do think some effort ought to be made to interrupt this mirror effect of our appearances, particularly the calabash pipes, said Dr. Glisteningly.

I have the corrective, said Dr. Glowingly as he pulled a derringer out of his breast pocket… Even of course as Dr. Glisteningly was also pulling a derringer out of his breast pocket…

# The Cottage in the Wood

He has built himself a cottage in a wood, near where the insect rubs its wings in song.

Yet, without measure, or a proper sense of scale, he has made the cottage too small. He realizes this when only his hand will fit through the door.

He tries the stairs to the second floor with his fingers, but his arm wedges in the entrance.

He wonders how he shall cook his dinner. He might get his fingers through the kitchen windows, but even so, the stove's too tiny to cook enough food; the pots are like thimbles and bottle caps.

He must also lie unsheltered in the night even though a tiny bed, with its covers turned down, waits for him in the cottage.

He curls himself around the cottage, listening to the insect that rubs its wings in song…

# The Double Bed

For a while now a woman has been turning into a double bed. She no longer wears regular clothes, but finds bedsheets and covers more fitting and comfortable to her new physical frame.

Her mother and father implore her not to encourage the seeming aspect by wearing bedclothes in the street.

The time was coming when she would no longer be able to leave the house, when she would have to remain in one of the bedrooms.

Her father removed the bed and said, I don't suppose you'll need a bed, because you are yourself a bed.

The family studied her to see just what style of bed she was becoming, so that they might buy matching furniture for her bedroom.

Her mother was afraid that she might be becoming some of that modern stuff.

Her father hoped she wouldn't be too old-fashioned, because that would seem too spinsterish.

The woman listens to her father and mother murmuring at night in the room next to hers. Her father murmuring in the dark, perhaps if she had gotten married there would have been a man in her double bed, and she wouldn't have to become a double bed all by herself. Oh, yes, it helps when you're married, it's such a lonely thing for a woman to become a double bed all by herself, murmurs her mother in the dark.

The woman thinks, it's a lot more comfortable, even in a double bed, to be alone.

And she lies alone in her double bed, the double bed she has become, staring up at the ceiling in the dark...

## The Large Thing

A large thing comes in.

Go out, Large Thing, says someone.

The Large Thing goes out, and comes in again.

Go out, Large Thing, and stay out, says someone.

The Large Thing goes out, and stays out.

Then that same someone who has been ordering the Large Thing out begins to be lonely, and says, come in, Large Thing.

But when the Large Thing is in, that same someone decides it would be better if the Large Thing would go out.

Go out, Large Thing, says this same someone.

The Large Thing goes out.

Oh, why did I say that? says the someone, who begins to be lonely again.

But meanwhile the Large Thing has come back in anyway.

Good, I was just about to call you back, says the same someone to the Large Thing.

# An Historical Breakfast

A man is bringing a cup of coffee to his face, tilting it to his mouth. It's historical, he thinks. He scratches his head: another historical event. He really ought to rest, he's making an awful lot of history this morning.

Oh my, now he's buttering toast, another piece of history is being made.

He wonders why it should have fallen on him to be so historical. Others probably just don't have it, he thinks, it is, after all, a talent.

He thinks one of his shoelaces needs tying. Oh well, another important historical event is about to take place. He just can't help it. Perhaps he's taking up too large an area of history? But he has to live, hasn't he? Toast needs buttering and he can't go around with one of his shoelaces needing to be tied, can he?

Certainly it's true, when the 20th century gets written in full it will be mainly about him. That's the way the cookie crumbles—ah, there's a phrase that'll be quoted for centuries to come.

Self-conscious? A little; how can one help it with all those yet-to-be-born eyes of the future watching him?

Uh oh, he feels another historical event coming... Ah, there it is, a cup of coffee approaching his face at the end of his arm. If only they could catch it on film, how much it would mean to the future.

Oops, spilled it all over his lap. One of those historical accidents that will influence the next thousand years; unpredictable, and really rather uncomfortable... But history is never easy, he thinks...

## The Liver Gag

A clown destroys a large liver which has been growing in his room for several years.

It began from a small blood stain on his wall, and has grown into a huge wet purple mattress bulging over his bed and make-up table. It is smothering his room, his elbow pokes into it when he sits to put his grease paint on; the covers of his bed are stuck under its weight.

He sticks the point of his funny parasol into it. It replies with a bloody cough.

He sticks the point of his funny parasol into it again, and it replies with a bloody fart.

Now he's into it, he's breaking it loose, prying it away from the wall with the handle of his funny parasol. It falls bleeding and breaking on everything; pieces of liver scattered all over the room…

Now dwarves are at his door shouting for the answer to the riddle of the Sphinx.

Please, I'm not ready, shouts the clown.

Then the fat lady's foot comes through the ceiling.

She must have eaten something…

The thin man is in the hall talking to the dwarves; he's going to try to squeeze through the keyhole.

Now the strong man is there, and he is offering to break the door down.

They have an elephant in the hall.

The circus manager is there, he's saying that if the clown doesn't open the door the building will have to be burned down.

The clown is wondering why the circus manager thinks the building will have to be burned down.

He hears the circus manager ordering someone to get some matches.

The dwarves are complaining that the clown hasn't answered the riddle of the Sphinx yet.

The fat lady's other foot comes through the ceiling. She must have eaten something else…

The thin man has forced one of his feet through the keyhole…

At the end, laughter and applause…

The clown curtsies, and begins to destroy a large liver again…

## Monkey-Overstreet's Lovely Surprise

The officers go into the monkey house and arrest monkey-Jim. The zoo keeper, trying to be as poignant as he can, says, why are you putting handcuffs on monkey-Jim?

I'm sorry, but we have an arrest warrant on monkey-Jim.

Oh, but that's not monkey-Jim, that's monkey-Charlie.

Well, where is monkey-Jim?

*That's* monkey-Jim—no, *that's* monkey-Jim… No, wait, *that* one's monkey-Jim… Sorry, that's monkey-Sam. There're too many monkeys, I can't tell which one is monkey-Jim.

Well, we'll just pick one at random, they all look alike, who's to know the difference?

But they all have names. If you take monkey-Elmer and call him monkey-Jim he'll think you're talking to somebody over his shoulder and won't confess. If you happen to take monkey-Overstreet the same thing'll happen.

Yes, that's true, say the officers, that's no fun. No one can expect monkey-Elmer or monkey-Overstreet to confess to monkey-Jim's crime… unless we torture them. Yeah, but that kind of a confession never seems sincere; sincerity is really important with confessions…

Well, officers, what can be done?

I guess we'll just have to torture monkey-Elmer…

You're not going to leave monkey-Overstreet out, are you?

The officers say among themselves, we can't leave monkey-Overstreet out, not after building up his hopes… Okay, they say, monkey-Overstreet can confess to monkey-Jim's crimes, too.

Oh, what a lovely surprise for monkey-Overstreet!

## The Pregnant Ones

A doctor is called to a house where a woman is about to have a baby. But when the doctor gets there he feels a little pregnant himself, and asks the woman's husband to call another doctor.

The woman's husband also looks a little bloated.

The doctor says, hey, you're not pregnant too, are you?

Well, Doctor, it's true, I have been feeling a little pregnant of late. Maybe I caught it from my wife?

When the second doctor arrives it's discovered that he's also pregnant...

And so the woman who is about to have a baby listens far into the night as three men argue about names for their own unborn children, which they fully expect will be sons...

from
*The Wounded Breakfast (1985)*
◊

## Our Poor Brains

A man had a brain. That's what they said he had. That his head was not just a storage of foetal hair.

They said whenever you are self-conscious you are self-conscious there.

They said who you think you are is known only there…

… Still, it's the reason we go to the madhouse, the reason we'll need a supervised environment… The walls are painted with calm colors there. And only insane laughter is allowed. That being considered the sincere symptom. All else is calm, all else is serious, because our poor brains are out of whack…

# How Things Will Be

*for James Tate*

... The kitchen will always be hungry then. The cupboard won't even find a bone.

The bedrooms will lie awake at night, blank-eyed against the whispery shuffle of hallways wandering back and forth, like blind mice looking for their eyes.

History in voluminous skirts waddled by knocking courage off the table.

The singing by the river turns out to be a radio plugged into the mouth of a corpse.

In a nearby field a butterfly is being folded up by a praying mantis into a small bright package.

... A tub of arthritic blood: Mother Hubbard kills the Sphinx.

In a dresser drawer a ruined city of hemorrhoids.

This... and the moon...

# The Way Things Are

There was a man who had too many mustaches. It began with the one on his upper lip, which he called his normal one.

He would say, this is my normal mustache.

But then he would take out another mustache and put it over his real mustache, saying, this is my normal one.

Then he would take out another mustache and put it over the other two and say, this one's normal.

And then another over the other three, saying, this one's abnormal.

And after several more layers he was asked why he wanted to have so many normal and abnormal mustaches.

He said, it's not that I want to, it's simply the way things are...

Then he took all the mustaches off. They like a rest, he murmured.

The first mustache, which we thought was real, was not.

We mentioned to him that we thought his first mustache was real.

He said, it is, all my mustaches are real; it's just that some of them are normal, and some of them are abnormal; it's simply the way things are...

## My Head

This is the street where my head lives, smoking cigarettes. I pass here and see it lying half asleep on a windowsill on my way to school where I study microbiology, which I finally give up because it all seems too small to have very much meaning in a world which I attempt to live in.

Then I begin my studies in advanced physics, which entails trying to understand atoms and subatomic particles. I give this up too when I finally realize that I have entered a world even smaller than microbiology.

I think then that I should become an astronomer and open myself to the largest view, but see only dots, which the professor says anyone of which might have taken millions, or perhaps billions, of years to reach only recently evolved optic nerves; and that in fact any star whose light we accept might be long perished, leaving only a long wistful string of light. And I wonder what this has to do with me or the world I attempt to live in. So I give up astronomy.

I come here now, into this street, looking up at my head lying half asleep on a windowsill, smoking cigarettes, blinking, and otherwise totally relaxed in the way men become when they have lost all hope...

# A Zoography

A man had a herd of miniature elephants. They were like wads of gray bubble gum; their trumpeting like the whistling of teakettles...

Also, he had a box of miniature cattle. When they lowed at sunset it was like the mewing of kittens...

He liked to stampede them on his bed...

In his closet a gigantic moth the size of a dwarf...

## The Paddlers' Song

    … Paddling for twenty years against the current. We haven't moved. If anything, we've lost.

    But the river closes the wounds of our displacements with neither scar nor pit.

    The shore was always there. We could have tied our boat and come as far.

    We might even have landed and put leaves together and had a roof, and watched the river with a pleasure grown aesthetic; the river that closes the wounds of our displacements with neither scar nor pit.

    We might have traveled inland to great cities to sit in drawing rooms; and against the mild baritone of cellos heard clever persons so describe the human condition as a place on a river, where men drown in the soft sounds of rushing water; the river that closes the wounds of our displacements with neither scar nor pit.

    We might even have flown (in the Twentieth Century men flew), to see the river of our struggle as one more thread from the great head of oceans… River that closes the wounds of our displacements with neither scar nor pit…

## The Park Bench

One evening a park bench followed an old man home.

The old man does not like anything to follow, particularly his undeserved reputation... He lives quietly, needing little, obscurity his shelter...

How a park bench should have found him out he doesn't know. Perhaps it was the musk of his rump...?

As he embraces the park bench in the darkness of his bedroom he asks, was it my rump, or my reputation? My sense of humor? Or more precisely, my abiding interest in skiing...?

# Slaughter Time in the Hills

*for Miroslav Holub*

*A three-hundred-pound man who is a son has been taking a mail-order course in herdsmanship. Now he is in his parents' room jumping up and down on his father's bed, almost throwing his father to the ceiling.*

Father: What is it? My God, what is it? Have you finally lost your mind? Is it time to call the police? We'll go through the floor! What do you want? What have I not fulfilled?

Son: I want to herd you.

Father: Oh, a little practice, huh? Why didn't you say so? Okay, just let us get our bathrobes and slippers.

*So the father and mother get up and put on their bathrobes and slippers, and allow their three-hundred-pound son to herd them.*

Father: Where to this time?

Son: Up into the grassy hills.

*So mother and father climb the stairs into the attic with their huge son behind them, poking them with his crook.*

Mother: I'm so tired of these midnight treks. It's either downstairs to the grassy valley, or into the attic for the grassy hills.

Father: The boy's learning a trade, it's the least we can do.

*Having reached the attic the father turns to the three-hundred pound man, who is his son:* Now what, down to the grassy valley of the kitchen for a midnight snack?

Son: No no, lesson six, *Slaughter Time in the Hills.*

Father: Slaughter time in the hills? We've never done that one before, how does it go?

Son: I cut your and mom's throats. A lot of blood. The grass sucks it down. You've been abusing the grass, now the grass is abusing you. Then I take your bathrobes like they were hides. I skin your bathrobes off you and leave your carcasses for the wolves and the crows, and for what more the grass can get, too...

Father: No no, I don't like that. That's no good at midnight. No, it's more like this, you herd two sheep into the hills. But they're not sheep, they're wolves in sheep's clothing. And when they get the herdsman alone in the hills they bite out his throat. A lot of blood. The grass sucks it down. You've been abusing the grass, now the grass is abusing you. When the wolves finish they leave your bones for the crows, and what more the grass can get, too...

Son: No no, the herdsman never gets killed, it's not the lesson!

Mother: He's right...

*So the three-hundred-pound son cuts his mother's and father's throats up in the grassy hills of the family house...*

## The Gift

A man put on a shoe and said to his dog, what more is there to do? Against this all things pale.

It is an achievement, certainly, said the dog, but what about your other shoe?

How many important achievements do you think I have in me? said the man.

Maybe you could put your hat on? It doesn't have any shoelaces, said the dog.

How very interesting, said the man, you know, you're beginning to open whole new worlds to me.

The dog felt flattered and its tail began to wag.

What are you wagging there? said the man.

You've made me happy, it must be my tail, said the dog.

Is that a great achievement? said the man.

I'm not usually aware of my tail, said the dog.

Ah, so then it's possible to do important things without even being aware that one is doing them. The list of my achievements must be incredible. If only I could be aware of them, that I might celebrate more fully... Ah, well, they're my unconscious gift to humanity...

# Edson's Mentality

A group of dead people are given electrical treatments. Their hair stands straight out from their heads. The doctor is pleased.

One of the corpses develops an erection. The doctor is pleased again.

These are signs of life! he cries.

A dead woman begins to blink violently, as if waking from a bad dream. This goes on for hours until one of the lids rips; the other breaks and slides off her cheek to the floor, still blinking, until the doctor steps on it, screaming, too much juice!

The corpse with the erection finally ejaculates.

The dead are producing life! cries the doctor.

He takes a smear of the ejaculate and puts it under a microscope, screaming, but the sperms are dead!

A nurse wipes his forehead and says, doctor, you're such a nice man, don't feel bad, yours are the sorrows of Dr. Frankenstein.

But, nurse, that's fiction.

Like this.

No no, this is real life, says the doctor.

No, says the nurse, Russell Edson is writing this.

No no, we are our own selves giving electrical treatments to the dead that they might live again! cries the doctor.

But we don't even live, says the nurse, so how can we make the dead, who, in fact, are not really dead, live?

Stop it, nurse, because you are running my life; won't feel like getting up in the morning anymore; nothing's real; drifting, I drift into fiction; from the window I see the trees of fiction, everything is turning to fiction; the *real* clouds are found to be only Edson's mentality...

I end up at the funny farm, and am told that this is just another of Edson's fictions—Lost, lost! I end up nutty as a fruitcake; maybe nuttier!

# The Inconvenienced Farmer

A farmer had just squeezed the juice out of a cow. He had the juice in a pail. He liked taking things away from animals—who says they have a right to them, anyway? They are really human things which the animals have stolen.

He enjoys cutting and pulling things out of the earth. He liked taking things away from the earth, too.

He thinks apples are too good for apple trees; potatoes much too good for the earth. And he wonders why the earth always has the good stuff.

He thinks rabbits have a nerve running away from him in the woods with all that good flesh on their bones, as if rabbits could think of a life other than that which serves man,

The stubborn wheat; he hates the wheat, which needs to be beaten and done-to to find its bread. The wheat ought just to surrender, and come up bread.

Why doesn't the steer come to man's door, mooing the dinner time; then fall apart in steaks and roasts?

His wife said, go down to the chicken house and get us some eggs.

Why don't those damn chickens lay their eggs up here; bad enough we've got to give them a house, that they can't come up here and deliver their eggs—good God, isn't it enough I'm willing to live on this earth, without all these inconveniences?!

The farmer grows cruel, when there are no eggs he shakes the chickens—damn you, where're my eggs. When the milk runs low, and the cow isn't ready, he kicks the cow in her ribs and cries, damn you, fill up your bag so I can squeeze you out!

Then one day, in the shadowy silences, a rabble of hooligan rabbits fell on the farmer and tickled him to death with their twitchy noses…

# With Sincerest Regrets

*for Charles Simic*

Like a monstrous snail, a toilet slides into a living room on a track of wet, demanding to be loved.

It is impossible, and we tender our sincerest regrets. In the book of the heart there is no mention made of plumbing.

And though we have spent our intimacy many times with you, you belong to an unfortunate reference, which we would rather not embrace...

The toilet slides away...

from
*The Tormented Mirror (2001)*
◊

## Sweet Tooth

A little girl made of sugar and spice and everything nice was eaten by someone with a sweet tooth the size of an elephant's tusk.

Ah, he said, this darn tooth, it's driving me nuts.

Then another voice is heard. It's the little girl's father who says, have you seen a little girl made of sugar and spice and everything nice?—Incidentally, what's that thing sticking out of your mouth like an elephant's tusk?

My sweet tooth, and it's really driving me nuts.

You ought to see a dentist.

But he might want to pull it, and I don't like people pulling at me. If they want to pull they should pull at their own pullables.

So true, said the little girl's father, people should pull at their own pullables and let other people's pullables alone. But still, he asked again, I wonder if you've seen a little girl made of sugar and spice and everything nice?

# The Key

An old woman was working her husband's beard into her shawl with her crocheting hook.

What's happening? said the sleepy old man blinking awake, his beard tangled in the old woman's shawl.

I think I've found the key to the universe, said the old woman showing the old man her crocheting hook. Look how it unlocks your beard and my shawl and relocks them as one. Why, you hardly tell where the one ends and the other begins.

But why is my secondary sexual characteristic becoming part secondary sexual characteristic and part shawl, even as a shawl becomes part shawl and part secondary sexual characteristic?

Because, while the key opens something, it must necessarily close something else …

# The Laws

If the rooster thinks he brings up the sun, and if the cow thinks she sets it with her lowing, what laws are broken?

Of course the cow is somewhat smarter than the rooster, but his convictions are stronger. The cow tends to be intellectually lazy. This makes the rooster appear to be quicker, but it's probably only his nerves. Roosters are born nervous wrecks. And still no laws are broken.

Should the rooster and the cow get married it has no legal force in human law. Nor has it sanction in natural law. So it is generally better for roosters to marry hens, and cows to marry bulls. Though neither has any legal force in human law, the law of nature does not discount it …

## The Position

They let me in. I went right up to the nursery and climbed into the crib and assumed the famous fetal position.

They didn't know what to make of it. They stood by the crib looking down at me.

They were young. This was their house. Instead of an infant, a grown man is in the nursery.

Of course they hadn't planned on anything like this. It never occurred to them that anything like this could happen. I had made my move. All I could do was to keep the position pretending to sleep …

## Baby Pianos

A piano had made a huge manure. Its handler hoped the lady of the house wouldn't notice.

But the lady of the house said, what is that huge darkness?

The piano just had a baby, said the handler.

But I don't see any keys, said the lady of the house. They come later, like baby teeth, said the handler.

Meanwhile the piano had dropped another huge manure.

What's that, cried the lady of the house, surely not another baby?

Twins, said the handler.

They look more like cannon balls than baby pianos, said the lady of the house.

The piano dropped another huge manure.

Triplets, smiled the handler …

# Pork Chop

As to what can be seen through a window …

   It depends. If the window is properly aimed one might see into another window just across the way.

   Then one sees a puppet working a pork chop like a surgeon operating with a scalpel, and putting pieces of the patient in his mouth.

   The puppet is having applesauce with his pork chop, just like me. I'm having applesauce with my pork chop, too …

# A Redundancy of Horses

There was a horse that had learned to ride other horses.

It's redundant, said the stable master's wife.

The stable master turned to his horse and said, it's redundant.

She said, and a horse riding a horse seems ...

Sensually endowed, said the stable master to his horse.

Will you stop repeating everything I say before I say it. That's an even worse redundancy than a horse riding a horse, she cried.

But ...

But, nothing, she cried.

Meanwhile, the horse had saddled up a mare, and was riding her away into a deep wood ...

## The Passion

First the butcher runs out of meat. Then he blushes. He blushes so deeply that his face begins to bleed.

He bows …

His customers applaud. One turning to another says, isn't it wonderful, he's run out of meat again.

And it proceeds. Now his face is covered with blood. The flies are just arriving.

Oh, those flies, they're spoiling everything, says one of the customers.

You can't blame them, they're pregnant and have no husbands, says another of the customers.

But they're spoiling it. And besides, they don't look all that pregnant.

The butcher's face is dead; black with crusted blood. He bows again. And the maternal flies begin to put their children into his face.

Someone whispers, is that part of it?

Of course, otherwise it wouldn't make any sense …

# Under Great Light Flooded Clouds

The horse is sticky. If you touch it, it sticks to your hands like chewing gum. The moon is all over the place.

A small village in the distance; dark brooding turtles with faint yellow eyes.

The horse, touching against its stall, leaves most of its rump. I scrape it off and pat it back, and start the horse out into the moonlight.

One of its hooves sticks to the floor, and becomes a long dark thread.

The moon is falling all over the place. In the sky great light flooded clouds are torn like bread.

I mount, and am away …

## Angels

They have little use. They are best as objects of torment.
No government cares what you do with them.

Like birds, and yet so human …
They mate by briefly looking at the other.
Their eggs are like white jellybeans.

Sometimes they have been said to inspire a man to do more with his life than he might have.
But what is there for a man to do with his life?

… They burn beautifully with a blue flame.
When they cry out it is like the screech of a tiny hinge; the cry of a bat. No one hears it …

# An Observer of Incindentality

A pebble lying on the ground. Another. A group, or colony of them …

They seem to have allowed a small piece of bark into their company. But have they? Has the small piece of bark merely intruded?

I suspect we may be in privilege of watching another example of the random …

The bodiless head of an ant. Is it a trophy, or is it just another of the possibilities found in collections falling together for no better reason than not being more widely scattered?

It's a question of spacing. How far things are allowed to be from one another while still calling themselves a group.

A question of time. The coincidence that allows pebbles and that small piece of bark to overlap with an ant's head.

Notwithstanding one, who watching this, also becomes attached to this grouping.

Does he intrude? Or is he simply accepted into an unconscious democracy of incidentality?

Perhaps it is simpler to say that for the most part he is simply unnoticed like any other incidentality.

Yet, if he would have one of those pebbles to more closely observe the incidental, it would expand out of its context into a monument of incidentality …

Conclusion: Incidentality is only theoretical. For once one becomes aware of it, it immediately moves to the center of one's attention, causing everything else to enter the incidental, including the observer of incidentality …

from
*The Rooster's Wife* (2005)
◊

# Fairytale

Behind every chicken is the story of a broken egg. And behind every broken egg is the story of a matron chicken. And behind every matron is another broken egg. . . .

Out of the distance into the foreground they come, Hansels and Gretels dropping egg shells as they come. . . .

## The Mare's Egg

The mare had layed an egg. It must have been the rooster made love to her.

Would you call what animals do making love?

He probably flew up to her chestnut rump and perched there with his bird feet, arching his posterior to the task.

But would you really call that making love?

Does it matter?

Of course, dear reader, whether animals can be said to make love or not, when the mare's egg opened a small pink Pegasus flew up and perched on the chestnut rump of its mother. . . .

## Evenings

There was a man who danced with his dog; his wife loving to sit evenings watching them. . . .

Suddenly she screams, Stop!

What happened? cries her husband skidding to a stop; the dog fainting.

I don't know, she says, Suddenly everything's reversed, now I don't love sitting evenings watching them.

Who?

That man who dances with a dog; didn't you see them? They were here just moments ago.

Then the man begins dancing with his dog again....

Suddenly his wife screams, It's reversed, now I love sitting evenings watching them.

Who? cries her husband skidding to a stop; the dog fainting.

That man who dances with a dog; didn't you see them? They were here just moments ago. . . .

# The Dog's Tail

An old woman was absentmindedly stirring a pot with a dog's tail.

When her husband asked her about the furry stirrer she said, It's the dog's tail, it came off in my hand.

When her husband asked her what she was stirring she said she didn't know, that all her thoughts were now for the dog's tail.

When her husband noticed that the dog was in the pot she said, Oh, is that where he is? I wondered where he got without his tail.

Her husband said, I'll bet he likes that, being stirred with his own tail. It's sort of like the tail wagging the dog.

The old woman said, I was just petting him, and it came off in my hand. I hope God wasn't looking.

Her husband suggested that perhaps it wasn't the dog's tail that broke off, but rather the dog that broke off....

# The Proud Citizen

An old man was proud that he had passed his years, as he had his breath and stools, without his having killed anyone.

He wondered if he might not report this to the police, hoping to be received with sirens and blinking lights of penal gratitude.

He would explain that he had had many opportunities, that it wasn't just laziness; that virtue without lure of sin hardly earns its name. . . .

## The Way

Now that you are falling down your stairway, what is it you have forgotten? Is it a window where last you saw the sky, that area above Monday morning's earth?

Now that each stair is whacking you back, breaking your calcium tree, you would have thought then to have walked more carefully. . . .

# Baby Doll

A dying old man is presented with a toy coffin made of cardboard.

A cardboard coffin? sighs the old man.

It's a funeral toy for little girls who like to play pretend death with their baby dolls.

But why cardboard? he sighs.

It's cheaper than wood, and good enough for make-believe funerals.

But what will my friends think when they see me laid out like a baby doll in a coffin made of cardboard?

You have no friends.

Then what will the God think when I arrive in a coffin made of cardboard?

There is no God....

# To Do No Harm

A doctor, keeping to his promise to do no harm, keeps a spare old man with a white beard in his medical closet in case someone should choke to death on a tongue depressor. Then he presents the spare old man to the patient's wife, in lieu of her husband, as another miracle of modern science—No extra charge for the beard.

Or, say he accidentally cooks a little girl to death with his x-ray machine, he can hide her under his white jacket and present the spare old man to the mother waiting in the waiting room, explaining that as he cooked her little girl she suddenly went into puberty, sprouting all kinds of secondary hair and nipples— Look, she even has a beard like a billy goat.

But even so, say the doctor should accidentally cut his own throat while shaving with his scalpel (this rarely happens), then he collapses into a pool of his own blood wondering if there is anything past death. If not, he simply fades into what he was before his mom and dad had groped each other in the dark.

And still no harm was done....

# At Sea

Two wifeless men at sea fishing for mermaids to wed. . . .

They wonder if their children will be fish. If daughters, they'd like them to be Emily Dickinsons born with water wings; nice shut-in types who write poetry and love their dads.

They're not against incest as long as it's kept in the family. Didn't Adam even make love to a piece of himself and create a whole species?

At last one of them says, Here we are at sea, ready to be fathers, and not one mermaid to accept our milt.

Perhaps we should just make love, as did Adam, to our ribs—The floating ones, which seems more than right for men who find themselves at sea. . . .

# New Prose About an Old Poem

One day an old poem is carried away by the wind. Its poet is relieved, now he won't have to be nice to it anymore.

The poem was always too good to throw away, yet, not good enough to publish.

It lived with him demanding to be reconsidered every so often.

But, even so, he sees that he's not to be rid of the old poem, the wind in reverse has returned it to his desk.

The old poem is glad to be home, and wants to be read again.

The poet reads it and realizes once again that it's too good to be thrown away. Perhaps, he thinks, he'll send it out in the next mail, knowing, of course, that he won't; and that he'll have to go on being nice to it for the rest of his life. . . .

# Let Us Consider

Let us consider the farmer who makes his straw hat his sweetheart; or the old woman who makes a floor lamp her son; or the young woman who has set herself the task of scraping her shadow off a wall. . . .

Let us consider the old woman who wore smoked cows' tongues for shoes and walked a meadow gathering cow chips in her apron; or a mirror grown dark with age that was given to a blind man who spent his nights looking into it, which saddened his mother, that her son should be so lost in vanity. . . .

Let us consider the man who fried roses for his dinner, whose kitchen smelled like a burning rose garden; or the man who disguised himself as a moth and ate his overcoat, and for dessert served himself a chilled fedora. . . .

## The Occasion

A large female presence is floated under a helium balloon to a sofa.

A man without legs walks into the room led by a blind seeing-eye dog.

Another, without a mouth, begins to sing a duet with someone shouting, Fire! on a bullhorn.

Still another, with his penis dangling like a caterpillar from his fly says, I'm sorry to interrupt this august occasion, but has anyone seen my pet condom? It crawled off my weewee and might be trying for a metamorphosis, even though butterflyhood has been promised to my weewee.

Meanwhile the helium balloon begins to tug at the large female presence like a sleepy child wanting to go home....

# Portrait of a Wrinkly Old Man with Nasty Genitals

There's this old grandpa dressed in a monkey suit, who wants to be known as grandpa monkey.

But you're a wrinkly old man with nasty genitals, says one of his descendants.

I have evolved, says the grandpa, Besides, I've fallen in love with a monkey maiden.

But you're too old to be in love.

I am not. I plan to live in a jungle with my monkey bride, and build a nest high in the trees and have love with her.

But you're too old to have love.

I am not. We plan to have love until the trees are filled with monkey children.

But you're just a wrinkly old man with nasty genitals wearing a monkey suit.

I am not. I'm a monkey who dressed himself in a monkey suit.

And with that he took off his monkey suit, and showed them that there was a monkey under his monkey suit.

Congratulations, you wrinkly old man with nasty genitals, you're a monkey!

Little did they know that the monkey under the first monkey suit was yet another monkey suit, and that under that was the same wrinkly old man with nasty genitals....

# Of Memory and Distance

It's a scientific fact that anyone entering the distance will grow smaller. Eventually becoming so small he might only be found with a telescope, or, for more intimacy, with a microscope. . . .

But there's a vanishing point, where anyone having penetrated the distance must disappear entirely without hope of his ever returning, leaving only a memory of his ever having been.

But then there is fiction, so that one is never really sure if it was someone who vanished into the end of seeing, or someone made of paper and ink. . . .

from
*See Jack* (2009)
◊

# Accidents

A man had accidentally gone to bed. When he noticed it he was terribly embarrassed, and said, Of course I'll marry you, please don't cry. And then he accidentally fell asleep.

Some hours later he found himself eating breakfast. And again embarrassed, said, Of course I'll pay all damages...

And then one day found himself on a psychiatrist's couch. And after promising the couch a nuptial alliance, said, Doctor, my life just seems one long accident, is there anything I can take for it?

Not to worry, smiled the psychiatrist, Sooner or later there's the fatal accident, which often leads to a total remission...

# The Applicant

A man looking for employment writes: Dear Employer, I would like to go to work for you. I'm not very good at anything, but I am able to sit quite pleasantly on comfortable furniture sipping whatever sippable you might offer. I wonder if you might have an opening?

The employer writes back: Dear Applicant, I'm afraid you're a bit overqualified. We'd not be able to pay you what you're obviously worth.

The man writes back: Dear Employer, All I ask is some comfortable furniture and some kind of a sippable. It would be my pleasure just to be getting out for a few hours every day.

The employer writes back: As of now consider yourself hired. We'll be ordering some furniture to fit your best comfort, and laying in a cellar of imported wines, not to mention a wet nurse, to quench your sipping needs.

Looking forward to greeting you.

Gratefully..."

# The Conversation

There was a woman whose face was a cow's milk bag, a pink pouch with four dugs pointing out of it...

A man with a little three-legged milking stool comes. She stoops and he begins to milk her face...

## The Eternal Worm

It all begins with a worm arriving too early, and trying to hurt me. At first I say, Cut it out. But the worm keeps trying to hurt me.

So I say, Hey, Funny Face, you're beginning to wear my patience thick—I mean, thin. Sometimes I mix them up. They're such relative terms.

So I say to the worm, Hey, Puke Head, you're wearing my patience thick—Thin, of course. But they're still relative terms. I mean, when does less thick become thin? Or thin, grown a little thicker, finally become thick?

So I say to the worm, Hey, Pickle Puss, my patience is getting thick—Thick, thin, what's the difference? When is thin so thin that it ceases to be? Or thick so thick that it owns everything in the universe?

So I say, Hey, Poker Face, I'm getting pretty sore, and my patience is growing thicker and thicker, even as the worm keeps trying to hurt me…

# The Gross Situation

A gross gentleman was soon joined by another gross gentleman. And they began to be very gross together.

Management began to feel that it was becoming too gross.

It's becoming too gross, said management.

What? said one of the gross gentlemen.

This area, said management.

Then we'd better move, said one of the gross gentlemen, Areas of unusual grossness make our thermometers read too high.

Oh, please, would you? said management, The street's a perfect place for it.

The street? whimpered one of the gross gentlemen, You forget how prone we are to fever.

The street would be fine, how good of you to think of it, said management, Certainly best to get it out of doors, more room for it there.

For what? growled one of the gross gentlemen.

For gross situations to develop into even grosser situations, said management.

The implication is just too gross, snarled one of the gross gentlemen as each of the gross gentlemen leaned from his chair and pulled a thermometer out of the crotch of his gross trousers.

A gross insult, huffed the other gross gentleman as each rose, fitting gross derbies and gloves to his person.

And besides, hissed one of the gross gentlemen, Our thermometers are reading far too high...

# The Hunger

A man puts his head in a hat. But the hat thinks he's feeding it, and begins to swallow his head.

No, no, Hat, I'm just completing my costume!

But his hat begins to suck his head like a huge mouth nursing a breast, sucking the milk of his thoughts into its crown.

But not only his hat, even his shoes are swallowing him. A two-headed creature turning his legs into the prongs of a tuning fork and vibrating him to death with road rhythms and footfalls; swallowing him down into the stomach of its distance.

But not only his shoes, but the rooms of his house are discovered to be the several stomachs of a monstrous cow where he paces back and forth like a cud of grass...

# A Lovely Cloud Poem to a Dear Friend

I looked into the sky and saw two clouds engaged in sexual intercourse like ghosts of giant whales moving through each other as if airships made of smoke...
I hope you like it,
Best wishes,
R

# The Man with a Sudden Desire to Bark at the Moon

He was advancing into featherhood. At first a little eiderdown in the middle of his chest. Then some good-sized feathers coming out of his elbows.

He wondered if there had ever been a bird in the family; some untalked-about ancestor. Perhaps an ostrich or a wren...

In any case he must prepare his mind to lose his teeth for a beak, his arms for wings, his human feet for the scaly toes of a bird...

But as he was developing into a bird he took a sudden turn, and started developing into a dog with a sudden desire to bark at the moon...

It makes no sense, he thought. Becoming a bird is one thing, but to stop becoming a bird after one is almost there, and to start becoming a dog, doesn't make any sense at all...

## Of the Night

A woman was trying to thread a needle to sew her husband's eyes to sleep. At first the idea was that of death. And then it was less. Finally becoming just another of the things one is put to do...

It was his idea, he had seen enough.

But can't you help me to thread the needle's eye? she said.

I've seen enough, he said.

But I cannot see to find the needle's eye, she said.

You must, he cried, Because I have seen enough.

But then she saw that the needle had gone to sleep, and closed its eye for the night...

## Portrait of a Realist

There is an old man who pukes metal. Today bedsprings. Yesterday, the iron maiden of Nuremberg.

His wife is more for cloth. Today she pukes used mummy wrappings. Yesterday, a teddy bear without a head.

Suddenly the old man pukes a battalion of lead soldiers. His wife upchucks a bundle of soiled diapers.

They have a son who's also a puker. But, unlike his parents, he pukes real puke…"

◊

# "No, And": Russell Edson's Poetry of Contradiction

Repetition and stasis, not progress, are the guiding principles of Russell Edson's mirror world. His poems end where they begin, having ruminated and gotten nowhere. Nothing ultimately changes in these mostly domestic scenes, though there are inciting events and there is some activity in the middle, but nothing is different when it all settles down again. Indecision guides these characters—choices are made, reversed, and then remade, only to be revised and reversed again.

Improv comedy students are taught to always respond to their scene partners with "yes, and...," meaning they should always affirm what their partner just said and add to it, rather than contradicting it. If one's partner says, "Hello, I am here to paint your house," you are supposed to respond with something like "Yes, the old place is looking rather drab lately," rather than something like, "No, you are a dentist," which would derail the unfolding sketch and stop the exchange of ideas between the two improvisers. Edson does not subscribe to this rule. Instead, he is obsessed with miscommunication; it is his bedrock truth. People don't listen to each other, are generally intent on fulfilling their own needs, and willfully ignorant of the needs of those around them. His characters constantly argue and contradict one another. In Edson's version of improv, "No, and..." is the rule: contradict and keep contradicting until the miscommunications have mounted so high that everyone gives up. This method wouldn't work on stage, but it makes for a marvelous, and marvelously dark, prose poem.

Edson was one of the definitive practitioners of the contemporary American prose poem. Charles Simic, in his beautiful Foreword, says that no one has yet offered a convincing definition of prose poetry. Nonetheless, permit me to make an attempt. Is a prose poem just a poem with no line breaks? If so, what can prose sentences and paragraphs do for a poem that lines can't? What is prose and what is poetry, and what are the supposed differences between them? The poet, critic, and translator Richard Howard, who was my graduate school mentor and friend, has a wonderfully useful and precise maxim for describing the difference between poetry and prose: "verse reverses, prose proceeds."

This concise and musical phrase summarizes what I believe to be one of the central truths about the nature of these two forms of writing: though made of the same basic stuff—letters, words, punctuation—once they take their shapes, they are actually different substances, like water and oil (though they do mix), or, perhaps, more like water and wood. They are composed of the same elements, but those elements are deployed so differently that the results can seem like distant cousins at best.

But what are they? First, we need a definition of "prose": it's the word on the street; the writing people talk in; the words on signs; and the stuff, beside images, that the Internet is made of. In itself, it's not scary (though lots of it piled up, say, in a big, fat book, might be). Reading prose, you might not even realize you're reading it.

Poetry, on the other hand, is always in the midst of defining itself, always justifying its existence, always trying to convince you it's there, not a ghost, and that you believe in it. Poetry isn't the lyrics to the song, but the words and music taken together. It's not the words on signs, but it's why signs work, because of icons, because you can understand what the whole sign—the words and images and colors taken together—means. You read poetry because you read poetry; it never lets you forget, because you're meant to be aware, the whole time, that you are reading a text about awareness—of words, sentences, lines, images, and the shifting meanings encoded in each.

To be fair, sometimes poetry and prose aren't always so different. But as readers, we come to each kind of writing with very different expectations, and here's where "verse reverses, prose proceeds" really does its descriptive magic.

What do we do when our eyes reach the end of a poem? When we get to the final line, to the stunning and surprising last word, the one that sends a lightning bolt back up through the body of the poem, changing the meaning, however subtly, of every word that's come before? We reread, of course. We go back up to the top and start climbing back down the page, gingerly or with wild abandon. Though, on this second descent, the poem is now relit by its conclusion; it means something new. Every word is redefined in this altered light. Verse reverses, meaning it points backward, ever remaking itself from end to beginning and then from beginning again to end.

Prose, meanwhile, proceeds—it points forward, its compass needle ever trained on what happens next: the coming scene, the event about to transpire, the sentence after this one. This is why prose has paragraphs, formless blocks of sentences in which it's irrelevant where the line breaks fall; we're typically meant to get on with it. Prose paragraphs are designed to draw our eye onward and downward, in a procession toward the end, that momentous (or precious, curious, cautious, mysterious, obvious) final sentence that lets us out of the piece of writing and back into the boring old world.

Of course, we often reread prose, but not usually because each sentence changes the sense of the ones that came before. In a poem, one never steps into the same sentence twice. In prose—fiction, memoir, even journalism—one can, but there are so many paragraphs still to read that one might as well keep stepping onward.

There are exceptions to all of the above, and often great writing—in poetry or prose—is great specifically because it breaks these rules. Edson's work is such an exception that proves the rule. But without stating the rules, and if writers didn't know them and to some extent agree on their virtue, they wouldn't be there to break. Prose is prose, until it's poetry, and vice versa.

There has always, of course, been verse that proceeds—think of *The Odyssey*— and prose that reverses—Aesop and Grimm, for example. But lately, prose that reverses has been flowing into the mainstream of literary writing, as writers are searching for ways to counter the endless scroll of the Internet, where prose goes to live forever as it dies, archived even as it's forgotten in the wake of the next post and the post after that. Fiction and nonfiction writers are desperate for poetry's staying power, for its demand that it be reborn as soon as it's been read.

Edson permitted himself to have it both ways, to write prose that reverses—each of his sentences simultaneously urges the reader forward into the action of Edson's stories in miniature, and also pulls the reader backward. Musical language, artfully loaded words, subtle twists in the plot, and all sorts of meaningful misdirections in Edson's work demand that we reread, that we never quite finish reading any of these poems, which are ever in the midst of revising themselves.

So how is Edson's work like prose, and how is it like poetry? In my fiction classes, I frequently teach a poem called "The Large Thing," from *The Reason Why the Closet Man Is Never Sad*, which seamlessly blends the qualities of poetry and prose:

> A large thing comes in.
> Go out, Large Thing, says someone.
> The Large Thing goes out, and comes in again.
> Go out, Large Thing, and stay out, says someone.
> The Large Thing goes out, and stays out.
> Then that same someone who has been ordering the Large Thing out begins to be lonely, and says, come in, Large Thing.
> But when the Large Thing is in, that same someone decides it would be better if the Large Thing would go out.
> Go out, Large Thing, says this same someone.
> The Large Thing goes out.
> Oh, why did I say that? says the someone, who begins to be lonely again.
> But meanwhile the Large Thing has come back in anyway.
> Good, I was just about to call you back, says the same someone to the Large Thing.

I love this little piece of writing, not least because I find the Large Thing adorable and pitiable, and because I rather love to hate the fickle someone. From a pedagogical standpoint, I love how this piece works as a kind of short story in miniature, utilizing the structural tools of rising and falling action, and a clearly delineated conflict, to create palatable tension. Of course, it is also a poem, using archetypal characters and imagery, as well as wordplay to accomplish its little task.

A statement in the present tense is often Edson's opening move. He likes the present tense—it lets him get away with anything, because it doesn't give us the opportunity or the hindsight to scrutinize this wily imagination. In the first two paragraphs—or are they lines?—we have the inciting action ("A large thing comes in") and the introduction of the central conflict ("Go out, Large Thing, says someone"). We are also introduced to our two main characters and learn immediately about their natures: the large thing is, we suspect, friendly, if imposing, and someone is grouchy and contrary. All of these aspects of the piece are characteristics of fiction, and were this piece not to have appeared in a book with the word poems on the cover, I would be perfectly comfortable saying we were wading into a tiny little story. But these characters are also archetypes, icons, their personalities encoded in their names. These are poetic qualities, the stuff ancient mariners are made of.

So then what happens? A conflict plays out until meaning is communicated. The Large Thing comes back in because it is in his nature, his character, to do so. Someone orders him out because that is his nature, though, like all good characters, he is ambivalent, wants two things at once: he "begins to be lonely," even though he seems to prize his privacy. Though perhaps what he prizes most of all is his ability to exert control over his companion.

When I teach this piece, I always ask my students who they like more, and how they really feel about someone. He strikes me as the kind of person who would kick his dog and then apologize and give him a treat, and then kick him again later. I find him somewhat despicable. And the Large Thing is a glutton for punishment, but also a deeply empathic friend, someone who understands someone better than someone understands himself. Many of my students feel the opposite, finding the Large Thing annoying and tactless, and someone a sort of victim.

But even having this conversation is evidence that my students and I are judging these characters as characters, that we've become aware of the fact that we are not reading a poem, but something else, something that plays on our sympathies, something that makes us view a world outside of ourselves, as much fiction asks us to do.

The climax of this little story occurs at the moment someone "begins to be lonely again," which is the apex of the story's conflict, when someone comes to understand his own ambivalence, and the reader gains wisdom and insight. That realization is why, in the last line or paragraph, someone says, "I was just about to call you back." This is the ironic dénouement,—despite someone's newfound insight, he is likely to repeat the pattern that the story illustrates.

This piece is an example of a deeply organic blending of the tools of poetry and prose, of forward narrative motion mixed with iconographic hitching back. "Ape," from Edson's 1973 collection *The Childhood of An Equestrian* is another sort of archetypal Edson poem, dense with the poet's favorite features: an ape, of course, Edson's imaginative spirit animal; a husband and wife whose conversation quickly degrades into a yelling match; the suggestion of perverse sexuality; and an ending in which the poem throws up its hands. "Ape" is funny, gross, and ultimately pretty sad, narrating a fundamental disconnect between two people who are sharing each other's lives. Marriage, for Edson, is always a prison, constrained and constraining, yet there's hardly ever the sense that anyone is motivated to try to escape.

Edson's "no, and..." template unfolds precisely in "Ape." The poem begins with mother nagging father (Edson also loves to poke fun at parents, who are inevitably in retreat from their active lives, lonely, and struggling with a sense of uselessness) about something he does not want to do—eat more ape. "I've had enough monkey," he retorts, setting up the terms of the exchange. From there, mother proceeds to offer a series of entreatments and arguments about the effort she's expended to make this dinner appetizing and appealing—she wants to feel her cooking is appreciated—until the poem climaxes with mother's backhanded confession: "I went to all the trouble to make onion rings for its fingers"; "Try a piece of its gum, I've stuffed its mouth with bread"; "Break one of the ears off, they're so crispy." Father replies each time with complaint and negation: "These aren't dinners, these are post-mortem dissections"; "Ugh, it looks like a mouth of vomit"; "I wish to hell you'd put underpants on these apes; even a jockstrap."

Then there is the extraordinary climactic paragraph, in which mother tries to throw off suspicion—"Are you saying I am in love with this vicious creature?"—only to confirm it in great detail: "after we had love on the kitchen floor I would put him in the oven, after breaking his head with a frying pan; and then serve him to my husband, that my husband might eat the evidence of my infidelity...." How should father reply? In this marriage, as in all of Edson's marriages, conflict is ultimately abandoned, not worth the trouble, unlikely to lead to anything that resembles resolution or connection.

Improv also teaches the idea of the game, in which scene partners play off of each other's ideas until they find a kind of exchange they can repeat, raising the stakes of the scene each time until a climax is reached. Edson does subscribe to this rule of comedy. Each time father negates mother, and each time she insists he go on eating, they raise the stakes, amplify the miscommunications, goad each other into increasing levels of frustration and hopelessness; the poem ends when the stakes have gotten so high that the argument must either end in a spectacular explosion or be abandoned. Edson usually chooses the latter, as he does here: "I'm just saying that I'm damn sick of ape every night."

In Edson's poems, people are always screaming at one another, and no one is listening to anyone else, though no one seems to expect to be listened to—Edson's conversations are more like shared primal screams. Until two thirds of the way through the poem, mother always "said" her statements. Father, however, at first "cried" and then "screamed," until mother feels that she too must raise her voice:

> I wish to hell you'd put underpants on these apes; even a jockstrap, screamed father.
> Father, how dare you insinuate that I see the ape as anything more than simple meat, screamed mother.
> Well, what's with this ribbon tied in a bow on its privates? screamed father.

This state of uninhibited frustration seems to be Edson's goal. It's as if each of his poems is a logic proof meant to show that attempts at communication always, eventually, lead to breakdown.

And what can we say about mother's proposed intercourse with the ape? It's certainly unpleasant to envision. But this kind of taboo sexuality is an essential ingredient of Edson's imagination. His poems begin so near to the edge of what is reasonable that they have almost nowhere to go but into the realm of the ridiculous, the perverted, the unconscionable.

Given that couples like this one are central characters in so many of Edson's pieces, it feels necessary to address for a moment the way Edson's conception of gender and marriage might strike today's readers. Edson's poems are drawn from a distinctly male imagination, and one formed in mid-Century. Gender roles are immutable, men go to work and complain, and women stay home and cook. Edson's poems are firmly rooted in a world before all the social advances of the last half century. The poems don't endorse that worldview—they satirize it—but neither do they allow for any any other conception of women and men. Envisioning a better world is beyond the purview of Edson's poetry.

Finally, "Ape" presents one of many versions of the microcosm that obsessed Edson, a circumscribed, domestic world in which two people torture each other passive aggressively until life is over while we laugh at them.

In his best poems, Edson is able to dramatize some of the nightmares of our increasingly nightmarish world, and to make us laugh about them, even if we're terrified. Of course, he's not throwing up his hands and simply saying that life's colossal ironies are merely funny. Edson is serious—his poems hold us accountable, even if they evince no hope that anything will ever get fixed. Edson's characters are people whose basic machinery is broken. They can't communicate. They won't listen, they won't shut up, and nothing improves. Nothing changes. But at least we can laugh—even if we're laughing at ourselves in Edson's tormented mirror.

**— Craig Morgan Teicher, 2022**

# Acknowledgments

Thank you to Mira Braneck for indispensable assistance in the preparation of this book.

Thank you to Peter Conners for sharing my excitement about this project, and to everyone at BOA Editions, Ltd. for another wonderful opportunity to make a book. Thank you to Brenda, as ever, for almost everything. Thank you to Lawrence Sikora, Russell Edson's friend and executor, for his help and enthusiasm for this project. Sandy Knight, thank you for another incredible cover. And thank you to Charles Simic for his beautiful Foreword.

Russell Edson dedicated each of his collections to his wife Frances, so it's only fitting that this book should be dedicated to her as well.

Cover photo of *Structure* by Russell Edson provided by Executor, Lawrence Sikora, LSikora1@mac.com.

Back cover photo of *Untitled Head* by Russell Edson provided by Executor, Lawrence Sikora, LSikora1@mac.com.

Portions of the *Afterward*, in a very different version, first appeared in *AWP Writer* under the title "Prose Reversing: On the Mechanics of the Lyric Essay."

The poems in this collection previously appeared in the following books:

*The Very Thing That Happens.* New York, New York: New Directions, 1964.
*What A Man Can See.* Penland, North Carolina: The Jargon Society, 1969.
*The Childhood of an Equestrian.* New York: Harper & Row, 1973.
*The Clam Theater.* Middletown, Connecticut: Wesleyan University Press, 1973.
*The Intuitive Journey and Other Works.* New York: Harper & Row, 1976.
*The Reason Why the Closet Man Is Never Sad.* Middletown, Connecticut: Wesleyan University Press, 1977.
*The Wounded Breakfast.* Middletown, Connecticut: Wesleyan University Press, 1985.
*The Tunnel: Selected Poems.* Oberlin, Ohio: Oberlin College Press, 1994.

*The Tormented Mirror.* Pittsburgh, Pennsylvania: University of Pittsburgh Press, 2001.

*The Rooster's Wife.* Rochester, New York: BOA Editions, Ltd., 2005.

*See Jack.* Pittsburgh, Pennsylvania: University of Pittsburgh Press, 2009.


"Accidents", "The Applicant", "The Conversation", "The Eternal Worm", "The Gross Situation", "The Hunger", "A Lovely Cloud Poem to a Dear Friend", "The Man with a Sudden Desire to Bark at the Moon", "Of the Night", and "Portrait of a Realist" from See Jack by Russell Edson, © 2009. Reprinted by permission of the University of Pittsburgh Press.

"Clouds," "How a Cow Comes to Live With Long Eared Ones," "Waiting for the Signal Man," "The Fetcher of Wood," "The Definition," "A Stone is Nobody's," "The Agent," "The Ancestral Mousetrap," "The Case," "The Clam Theater," "The Family Monkey," "The Floor," "The Mental Desert," "Oh My God, "I'll Never Get Home," "Antimatter," "Ape," "The Dainty One," "The Further Adventures of Martha George," "The Toy-Maker," "How Things Are Turning Out," "The Intuitive Journey," "Counting Sheep," "The Abyss," "The Feet of the Fat Man," "Mr & Mrs Duck Dinner," "The Hemorrhoid Epidemic," "The Intuitive Journey," "The Marionettes of Distant Masters," "Grass," "The Dogs Dinner," "The Cliff," "The Reason Why The Closet-Man Is Never Sad," "The Coincidental Association," "The Cottage in the Wood," "An Historical Breakfast," "The Large Thing," "How Things Will Be," "The Way Things Are," "My Head," "A Zoography," "The Paddlers' Song," and "With Sincerest Regrets" from The Tunnel: Selected Poems of Russell Edson. Copyright © 1964, 1969, 1973, 1977, 1985, 1986, 1994 by Russell Edson. Reprinted with the permission of Oberlin College Press. All rights reserved.

"Sweet Tooth", "The Key", "The Laws", "The Position", 'Baby Pianos", "Pork Chop", "A Redundancy of Horses", "The Passion", "Under Great Light Flooded Clouds", "Angels", and "An Observer of Incidentality" from The Tormented Mirror: Poems by Russell Edson, © 2001. Reprinted by permission of the University of Pittsburgh Press.

# About the Author

**Russell Edson** (1935–2014) was the author of many books of prose poems, including *The Very Thing That Happens*, *The Reason Why the Closet Man Is Never Sad*, *The Rooster's Wife*, and *See Jack*. He is also the author of a collection of plays, *The Falling Sickness*, and the novels *Gulping's Recital* and *The Song of Percival Peacock*. He lived in Darien, Connecticut.

**Craig Morgan Teicher** is the author of four poetry collections, including *Welcome to Sonnetville, New Jersey* and *The Trembling Answers*, which won the 2017 Lenore Marshall Poetry Prize from the Academy of American Poets. He is also the author of the essay collection *We Begin in Gladness: How Poets Progress* and the editor of *Once and For All: The Best of Delmore Schwartz*. He lives in New Jersey with his family.

# BOA Editions, Ltd.
## American Poets Continuum Series

# Colophon

BOA Editions, Ltd., a not-for-profit publisher of poetry and other literary works, fosters readership and appreciation of contemporary literature. By identifying, cultivating, and publishing both new and established poets and selecting authors of unique literary talent, BOA brings high-quality literature to the public.

Support for this effort comes from the sale of its publications, grant funding, and private donations.

*The publication of this book is made possible, in part, by the special support of the following individuals:*

Anonymous (x2)
Angela Bonazinga & Catherine Lewis
Jennifer Cathy, *in memory of Angelina Guggino*
Peter Conners
Chris Dahl, *in memory of Sandy McClatchy*
Susan DeWitt Davie
David J. Fraher, *in memory of Al Poulin*
Bonnie Garner
James Long Hale
Margaret Heminway
Kathleen Holcombe
Nora A. Jones
Jack & Gail Langerak
Paul LeFerriere & Dorrie Parini
John & Barbara Lovenheim
Richard Margolis & Sherry Phillips
Frances Marx
Joe McElveney
Boo Poulin
Deborah Ronnen
Sue Stewart, *in memory of Steven L. Raymond*
Rob Tortorella
Robert Thomas
Lee Upton
William Waddell & Linda Rubel